AS SHE RECOVERS

Angela Shepherd

As She Recovers

This book is a creative nonfiction story about an experience in a treatment center. Though it is based on real life experiences, it is the compilation of stories and does not reflect on any one individual. The author in no way represents any company, corporation, or brand.

ISBN 979-8-218-24075-2

Published by:
Sono Publishing
Email: https: angela-shepherd.com
Social: angela shepherd

Cover Design: Lulu Lovering Shepherd
Lulu Lovering.com

Formatting: Polgarus Studio

Have you ever been brought to your knees by life, unsure of how to get up, again? Many of us turn to something to distract or numb from the inevitable work of……change.

Addiction is a destructive accelerant, often fueled by trauma, mental health, loss, and isolation.
Substances are a symptom of a deeper longing to connect.
As She Recovers is the story of the acceptance, honesty, courage, of rising up, together.
Something *is* different here, in this healing house where true connections are made; connection to self, genuine connections to others, spiritual connections, and the restorative Power of Unity.

She couldn't run any longer, but couldn't stop.
She couldn't go back and didn't know how to go forward.
She had promised herself She would stop, tomorrow, for her little Emma.
But active addiction is a runaway train with no regard for today, or tomorrow.
How could the solution be living with 40 women in a Cape Cod mansion by the sea?
How could She live another day without Emma?
How?

Struggling to accept her identity as a person in need of Recovery, She remains nameless until her moment of grace when Hope is introduced.
Her transformation a byproduct of the unconditional love of the staff and peers She meets at the center.

As She Recovers is a passage from survival to living through the gates of change.
Experience resilience from all angles of discomfort, surrender, growth, strength, and joy.
Within the mystery of the miracle of community, we do recover.

Contents

We acquire the strength we have overcome.

– Ralph Waldo Emerson

This book is dedicated to the courageous women of the healing house; residents, staff and our village of supporters, Sisters One and All

MESSAGE TO THE READER

"What if I do recover?" This question was asked by a young woman in treatment. She was afraid she would be stuck in active addiction, while terrified of what life in recovery might be like without a way to numb the pain. For many people, this unnerving fear of failure, as well as the unknowns of success, blocks the path forward and upward. Active addiction (when someone is actively using substances without regard to negative consequences) masquerades as "being in control" for a period of time, until it's too late. You become trapped physically, mentally, and spiritually in its controlling grips. Amongst the many routes to recovery is the longstanding Big Book of *Alcoholics Anonymous.* In Chapter Five, it states, "Remember we deal with alcohol – cunning, baffling, and powerful. Without *help* (emphasis mine) it is too much for us." What I can tell you – as a person in long-term recovery and with a 25-year career running a substance disorder residential program – is that help is available and people do recover!

Everyone is brought to their knees by life at some point – be it addiction, illness, loss, or trauma. Addiction is particularly effective at bringing people to their knees. The need to change becomes very evident. The choice is how do we get back up and change? The act of change presents a unique blend of components – the need for honesty, acceptance, motivation, and most importantly, a support network. Addiction is not about the pleasurable effects of substances, but the user's inability to connect in healthy ways with themselves and other human beings. Foundations of support and connection are why residential treatment centers are effective in facilitating change. British-Swiss journalist Johann Hari echoes a theme that 21st-century addiction specialists have proposed for years, "The opposite of addiction is not sobriety, it is connection."

I had the blessing, challenge, grace, and calling for over 25 years to work amongst women at the threshold. Alongside these brave souls, I served and led a team of dedicated professionals as we guided women through their initial journey back to life, to a will to live, and to grow. As the Program Director, I built community-healing connections through transparency, integrity, innovation, and love. The staff met women where they were – in their darkest moments – and helped them rekindle their will to live. I have woven *all* women into this memoir, where their stories touched, challenged, and created transformation. One step and one day at a time.

Patients in our program would say, "There is magic in the walls here." The *magic* was in the authentic connections they made with each other, with the staff, the community, and eventually their families. They were able – many for the first time in their lives – to be seen, heard, and understood for exactly who they were at that moment. By nature, the inherently messy human condition is not something as openly talked about in our culture as it should be. Freedom and connection begin to develop as women shed their layers of guilt, shame, fear, insecurity, and disconnection. As this process unfolds, our staff would see sparks of life coming back in women's eyes. It was magic. It was sacred. It was joyous even amidst the wreckage of addiction.

As a word lover, I have always been fascinated with the word *recovery*. I'll sum up one of my favorite definitions: the regaining of possibility, of something lost or taken away. What I witnessed every day was women reclaiming, regaining, and restoring their lives. Recovery – in its purest form – is a return to self. Within the innate messy nature of life, beauty exists in our shared vulnerability and frailty, and once revealed, it shines. We stand, we stand up, we stand tall, we stand together, reclaiming that which was lost along the road of addiction. I personally spent the first 23 years of my life unknowingly searching for my soul family. This lost wandering brought me to my knees, humbled and hopeless. I was led to a life-saving fellowship overflowing with people who spoke the truth, no matter how harsh or challenging it seemed. The fellowship I found within a healing house had one purpose: to help those suffering and lost. Women like me entered the halls, church basements, and treatment centers drained of our life force. Shrouds of shame, guilt, denial, anger, and sorrow insulated us from accepting help. Yet we were seen, accepted, supported and loved until we could lift our heads up and begin to see our reflection in those smiles as they repeated, "Keep coming. It gets better." In the following 25 years, I dedicated my life to helping others find the same light of hope and strength within this healing house. I led with humility and a fierce commitment to finding innovative ways to reach each individual who came to us. I witnessed strength, bravery, joy, sorrow, inspiration and love beyond measure. I believe that the message of the human spirit – when it rises from the depths of darkness into the light of healing and reconnection – must be shared.

As She Recovers is one woman's journey through a healing house. "She" has lost her identity to addiction. "She" is hesitant and afraid of labeling herself as an addict and alcoholic for fear that nothing else is left of her. "She" will remain anonymous to the reader until – through connection with others and herself – she finally claims her seat in recovery and her new identity as "Hope." This pronoun-to-name choice is deliberate for the purpose of this narrative. Her story is inspired by countless women whose names remain anonymous. She is all of them. She will take you along her journey where you will experience intertwined and layered stories of women being restored through a healing community, *as she recovers*.

PROLOGUE

Dear Emma, How could this have happened? It wasn't that bad. I was going to stop, to change, but I couldn't stop. Why couldn't I stop? It makes no sense. I'm not an alcoholic; I can't be. I'm your Mom. I just lost control. I love you more than anything. I can't be away from you. Don't cry, baby. I promise, I'll stop. I will. Please, please, if there is a God or anything out there, please.

I'm sitting in the backyard and can't go back in. You are gone, but your toys are still all over the house. Sitting under our favorite tree, I can't imagine how its leaves are innocently blowing in the wind while my heart breaks and the world stops, without you. Could the wind possibly know that my life is over? It mustn't because it just keeps blowing, moving through the trees, like nothing happened. Maybe if I keep writing to you, you will come back to me.

What have I done?

I love you,
Mumma

I Am Here

What if walking up these four large granite steps right now would be the first step to recovering pieces long lost, stolen, surrendered by her own choices?

She paused at the first step. Thick ivy climbed the side of the stately mansion. Fall leaves were yellowing. She vaguely knew Alcoholics Anonymous taught Twelve Steps to recovery, yet only four led up to the front doors of this place. She knew these four steps were the first to get back her daughter. Feet heavy with the despair of failure, She made her way up, wondering if she could face herself again, this time. But this time was worse.

This time it wasn't just letting herself or her family down. She had promised to never let her sweet, innocent Emma down. Then the promise was broken. She broke Emma's heart and shattered her own. "This is my last chance," She spoke under her breath.

She reached for the large stone pillar beside her for support. Her ride had left. No turning back now. She looked up at the house looming above her. The stiff October breeze rustled the leaves beneath her feet and stung her broken spirit. She closed her eyes, soaking in the earthy Autumn air, trying to feel something besides panic.

She pulled her hood up around her neck; it was much colder here. The detox case manager had made it sound like a vacation, "Go to Cape Cod for a few months. It's a beautiful spot."

Feeling isolated and stuck, so far away from Emma, She contemplated calling her ride back before the staff here confiscated her cell phone; but as the wind blew across her face, She realized she didn't even know where her daughter was now.

"Welcome to Everson." A warm hand descended on her wrist. "I'm Judy, the House Manager." The woman led her through the front door. Slowly, her trance wore off, as they entered the foyer

Smiling faces welcomed her with a warmth that She just couldn't recognize. They must be faking, or worse yet, lying to her like everyone else had. Surely they knew of the destruction that had brought her here. She could not distinguish the staff from the residents through their bright eyes and oddly-thick smiles. Did they expect her to fake it too and pretend everything was actually okay?

She thought of her sweet little Emma. *Should I even keep breathing?* She wondered.

Someone yelled, "Hey Judy, why did my room get a low score today?"

"The top of your dresser was messy," Judy replied, carrying on as if everything was normal.

"Aw, c'mon, give me a break, Juds." The voice faded in the background, as Judy continued to guide her through the house.

"Group time," Judy cheerily hollered into the dining room. A blur of women emerged. Some smiled and welcomed her as they walked by, all passing through the foyer and heading into what looked like a large living room. *Welcome. Hi, are you new? You're going to love it here!*

Judy led her into the main office and smiled, "Now, we are going to get to know each other."

Judy launched into more information about the program than She could possibly absorb – the schedule, rules, expectations, and countless other useless rattling words. Judy calmly went on and on. She could not believe it, yet felt somewhat comforted by it. Soon, She was distracted by the smell of coffee and brownies warming the air. Judy explained that the recovery aid staff needed to go through her belongings, then introduced her to her "Big Sister."

Here we go. I'm out of here. She told herself, imagining her escape route. But tired and hungry, She figured dinner would come first.

Big Sister, who had only been there three weeks, bounced towards her, "Welcome to Everson!" With a big obnoxious smile, she said, "You can call me Big Sis!"

Big Sis wouldn't stop talking about how much better she felt since being here. "This place is different."

It sure is, She thought, *pretty sure this is where the loonies land.* Big Sis was easily ten years younger than her. Her black hair piled atop her head and her zig-zag yoga pants could not have done terrible things. *How could she possibly be so cheery,* She wondered, looking into Big Sis's bright brown eyes. Big Sis didn't look away but met her look with a steady one of her own. In a flash of a moment, She felt seen in a way she never had, and it scared her. She wanted to run.

"Everyone struggles in the beginning," Big Sis nodded, as if she'd read her mind, and she handed her a brownie. Her cascade of encouraging words began to fade slowly into the background amidst the pure pleasure of the warm fudgy brownie.

She wondered what was in it for this woman, this Big Sis. Then came her very serious lecture about moving your "recovery rock" every morning from the "addiction bowl" at the bottom of the stairs to the "recovery bowl" in the foyer. She was told she would paint her own recovery rock in the art room during free time that afternoon and then put it in the recovery bowl tomorrow.

"It's an outward sign that we are making a decision to be in recovery each and every day," Big Sis gave her an unsolicited hug. "After all, it's one day at a time."

She was convinced this place was some sort of cult and started looking for the guy handing out the crazy Kool-Aid.

Judy and Big Sis brought her belongings up the winding staircase to Room 23, where two other women were listening to music. They looked up long enough to introduce themselves as Tina and Jen, then went back to their music.

Finally, She thought. *Someone else who doesn't seem to give a shit.*

The beds were close together, only a few feet apart. She wasn't planning on staying here, so she didn't care about other women sharing her room.

"That's your bureau," Judy said, pointing to the roomy corner of the closet that was bigger than her room at home. "Dinner is at 4:45 and the Commitment Meeting is at 7:30. My shift ends at 4:00 pm and I will introduce you to the

Recovery Aid staff working tonight before I leave."

She wanted to tell Judy to stop treating her like a child, though she felt like one at the moment.

"Don't worry, Judy's kind of like the House Mom and treats everyone like that," Tina said, her rough smoker's voice crackling as she laughed.

She sat on her bed across from a Victorian-styled, green-tiled fireplace, legs dangling like a kid from the tall bed frame. *What is this place?* She thought. A gold-framed picture of two leaning bikes on a bridge overlooking the ocean looked like something from a fancy hotel. *This is just bizarre*, She thought. *I've never been to a rehab like this before.*

Judy knocked and flung the door open again, with a book in her hand, "I almost forgot to give you a journal. Writing can be helpful in many ways in early recovery. There are things you may not be able to talk about that you could write about and start working your way through."

She nodded and took the flowered journal from Judy, not wanting to hear anything more today. She thought of the soft leather tree-of-life journal her sister Brenda had given her the first time she had checked in for treatment three years ago, before really wrecking her life. She actually had the leather journal in her bag. She had carried it everywhere in hopes of writing again, but her life had gotten too dark to write upon its clean white pages.

"Let's finish the house tour," Big Sis suggested, hooking her arm through hers. She normally would have resisted but just didn't have the energy.

"If you live on the second floor you're not supposed to go up the third floor, but it's cool so we'll take a quick look," Big Sis said, leading her up the narrow staircase. "You can see the ocean from up here; it's really cool."

They crossed a windy breezeway between the two buildings. "It's always windy in this spot. Ocean breeze, as Judy calls it." Big Sis said, then pointed towards the backyard, identifying different parts of the building around it. "Staff offices and the med room," Big Sis said, as if she was on the payroll. Then they walked into a smaller annex building.

She looked into a cozy living room and saw four young mothers and babies. She was curious that they all seemed to have their visitation times at the same time.

Big Sis leaned in, "This is where the Moms and babies live."

"Live?" She asked in shock. Nobody had told her that there were mothers and babies living together in this program. She felt tricked and freaked out, "No, no. I can't be here with babies. Nobody told me you could have babies here." She whispered, as her heart dropped, churning in her stomach.

Clueless as ever, Big Sis asked, "Do you have kids?"

She nodded slowly, feeling numb as Big Sis mentioned her own son who was living at her home with her Mom. "Not my first choice since she raised me and that didn't turn out so good, but it's better than him being in a foster home."

One of the mothers walked towards them with a baby on her hip and introduced herself, "Hi, I'm Ashley and this is my daughter, Kayla."

She choked out a hello and tried to tell Ashley that her daughter was beautiful, but had to run out of the building. Embarrassed by her tears, She leaned herself into the side of the building where nobody could see her.

Judy found her later. She came around the corner, calmly asking, "Are you alright?"

Head in her hands and back against the wall, She whimpered, "I need to leave. I can't stay here. Can you get my things?" *My things*, She thought. *What good are my things if I don't have my Emma?* "Never mind, it doesn't even matter. I just need my phone to call for a ride." She sniffled.

Judy handed her a tissue, "The first few days are hard for everyone. It's too much to try and absorb all at once."

She looked up slowly, insisting, "It's not that. I can't be here with babies. I can't deal with a constant reminder that I am not with my daughter."

"How old is your daughter and what's her name?"

"Emma, she's only three." Her heart broke with each word.

"And where is Emma?"

"In foster care. I did that to her." She grimaced through the words and sank to the ground at the weight of this reality. Judy knelt down beside her in the dirt and listened. "What if I'm too far gone and can't get sober? If I can't be with Emma, I can't be here. I can't be on this planet," She cried.

Judy was quiet until She looked up from the ground.

"I can't even imagine how painful this is," Judy said. "But what I can tell you is that other women in this house have felt the pain you are feeling, being separated from their children. Together, with support, they are able to face this gut-wrenching pain, survive, and begin to heal."

"But Emma doesn't know where I am," She cried. "She must be so afraid."

"Three-year-old children don't feel emotion the same way we do. Developmentally, she is more concrete and does not feel the abandonment you feel," Judy assured her. "I'm sure Emma is being taken care of and, hopefully, you will see her soon."

Judy stood up, dusted off, and reached out a hand. She took Judy's hand. Standing there in her blue-and-white striped shirt and sneakers, Judy was short but seemed larger than life. Maybe it was all of the information Judy carried that had made her seem that way.

"Do you like my tennis shoes?" Judy asked with a smile.

"What?" She mumbled.

"My tennis shoes, you were staring at them for a while."

"You mean sneakers? No… I'm just so tired … well, yes … I do like your sneakers, but honestly, I was just spacing out."

"I'm from the Midwest. We call sneakers tennis shoes," Judy continued with an arm around her shoulder. "It's been a rough day. Let's go up to your room so you can get some rest before dinner." She didn't even care that two other women were in her room. She collapsed on the bed exhausted and worn. Just as she was nodding off, Jen, her new roommate, said quietly, "It gets better."

She gazed bleary-eyed at the small flame-shaped lights over the fireplace mantle and drifted off to sleep.

Moments later, Big Sis came bouncing in the room to wake her up, "Let's go, dinner time! It's my favorite too! Meatloaf!"

She could smell the warmth of a home-cooked meal wafting in through the open door and was suddenly ravenous. She stood up to a pounding headache. Walking down the long winding staircase to the dining room, She noticed the plush green carpet beneath her feet for the first time. Pretty flowers and white vines sprawled along the dark green forest-like carpet. It reminded her of the vines wrapped around the house and the front pillars, green but starting to yellow, slowly climbing towards the sky. She felt like a vine too, but without anything to hold onto.

The dietary aid serving dinner introduced herself, "I'm Patty. Welcome. I'm so happy to meet you." She handed her an overflowing plate with meatloaf, mashed potatoes, gravy and corn.

Big Sis and two more women were sitting at a table and going on and on about what meeting they were trying to get to tonight. She could only focus on the amazing gravy. She couldn't remember the last time she'd had a comforting meal and picked up her fork.

The last specks of dusk-colored light poured in through the old-fashioned, large glass doors. Its crystal doorknobs cast little rainbows across the wall. Time seemed to slow and quiet down despite the talking and laughing coming from women as they gathered around the tables, filling up the dining room. It seemed so normal as she finished her plate. *But what the hell is normal?* She wearily made her way back up to her room and waited for her first meeting.

"7:00 pm. Almost time for the meeting!" An older, recovery aid named Shirley poked her curly head through her bedroom door.

She rolled over with no intention of getting up; but found that she was thirsty, surprisingly hungry again, and wanted a smoke.

"How's your first day been so far?" Shirley hovered at the door.

She had no words. Just blank, tired, and worn out.

"Don't worry." Shirley attempted to assure her, "Most of the RA staff are in recovery too. We get it; the beginning is the toughest part. Just keep showing up, as they say. Bring the body and the mind and spirit will follow. I'm here to help you show up."

She wanted to be irritated but Shirley's direct approach felt somehow comforting.

"C'mon, let's head downstairs," Shirley said, motioning towards the door.

She looked up from Shirley's orthopedic brown shoes to her curly gray hair and confident expression. *Could this woman actually know how shitty I feel*? She wondered.

"Don't let fear hold you back," Shirley said, as if reading her mind. "Your thinking got you into this mess. Give us a chance to show you a different way."

"Can I just listen?" She asked, yawning and wishing she could crawl back under the covers.

"Sure thing," Shirley said, walking into the hall as if to pull her along. She hollered down the hall at the rest of the residents, "Everyone at the bottom of the stairs, we're going outside. If you're smoking, you have five minutes till the meeting in the dining room!"

She finally wandered down the long wooden stairway to the backyard, grumbling about the rules. Judy had already given her an earful. *Enough already.* She took a seat as far back in the yard as possible to get some space from it all. The grass was damp from a recent light rain. The full moon reflected off the back of the big house and it did look beautiful. *What a strange place,* She thought as the group of women at the bottom of the stairs laughed and goofed around. *How can they seem so genuinely happy?* She couldn't understand why they weren't miserable. But curiosity began to gain on feelings of anger.

Six overly-cheery women drove up to the house for some sort of Commitment Meeting. They introduced themselves as Everson alumni.

Now maybe the real scam will be revealed and they'll be exposed for all of this useless cheeriness. Forty women living together has to be pure insanity. She decided to take a seat closer so she could pick things apart. *These unrealistically upbeat women came out on a rainy night to cram into a crowded space with all these other women to talk?* She pulled up her hoodie and sat with her arms and legs tightly crossed, just in case anyone had any ideas of talking to her. She was pondering her escape when women began to share.

"My name is Rebecca and I am an alcoholic and addict." A tall blonde woman belted out with pride. *Ridiculous.*

Another woman named Jess introduced herself as the one who would be chairing the meeting tonight, and then she went on to speak of things that were unspeakable, but she had a sense of joy. *Well, that makes no sense.*

Another woman shared how things that had happened to her had led to her self-destruction and revolt against life. *You're basically telling my story. These things are horrible. I know I am horrible.*

She eased her hood down and saw others nodding along as women spoke of their nightmare stories and the lives they had rebuilt in recovery. When women caught her eye, they smiled at her. *How can you all sit here with smiles on your faces? Don't you know all these terrible things have happened to me?*

Something faintly resembling her own quiet spirit whispered, *They do know.*

At the end of the meeting, Jess asked if anyone had any "burning desires." *Getting out of this place*, She thought and smirked to herself. One of the women raised her hand and talked about struggling to stay in the program because her boyfriend had just gotten out of jail. Jess thanked her and asked if anyone else wanted to share.

She thought it was odd that Jess didn't address the woman's concern. *Figures*, She thought, silently judging Jess's knock-off Ugg boots and fuzzy pink vest. *Who wears a vest nowadays*?

Kate – an Everson alumnus who had shared about having gotten custody of her kids back five years ago – approached her after the meeting, gave her phone number, and, before walking away, said, "Hang in there. It gets better, I promise."

It gets better. The same words her roommate had spoken earlier. She felt, for a moment, like maybe some of the women here understood what she was going through. It felt comforting, but not if she had to get up and label herself an alcoholic or addict. *Nope, not doing that.*

"Snack time," Shirley yelled from the main office.

"What kind of a place tells us when to have a snack?" She quipped aloud.

She sat amongst the women who were busily laughing and talking loudly, slurping down the last of her chocolate mousse. *Emma loves chocolate mousse,* She thought, softening. Her anger was replaced with intense aching. *My sweet Emma.* She decided to get some sleep and leave first thing in the morning.

She pitched herself back up the winding stairs to escape the day and crashed on her bed again. Her roommate piped up, "Don't forget to start your autobiography!"

Everyone can't be this cheery. I'll see their true colors in the morning. She shook her head as her roommates headed out again for another smoke. *For now, I have the room to myself. And for tonight, I am here.*

The last three words rang through her mind and her writer's spirit took its first breath in years. Instead of sleeping, her hand fumbled through her packed bags and found the tree-of-life journal that her sister had given her. She sat up, smoothed the soft leather cover, breathed in the smell of the fresh paper, and her heart warmed. Pen in hand, She imagined writing the first three words, *I am here*. Opening the cover, harshly-scribbled ink on the first page leaped at her. She forgot she had written in a haze that night, when Emma was taken by the police. She'd sat outside in the yard, unable to go into her empty house, and penned a desperate, heartbroken letter to her daughter. She sat on her single twin bed, frozen in front of the green tile fireplace, on the second floor of an ivy-covered mansion, somewhere by the sea, in a town unfamiliar to her. The journal fell to the floor, the first page splayed open. Her breath caught sharply in her chest. *There it is, my worst moment stained across the white page.*

What seemed like an hour later, almost audibly, the three words told to her over and over since her arrival here broke through her memory. *It gets better.*

She picked up her tree-of-life journal, turned the page past her first desperate words to her daughter, and wrote.

Dear Emma, I Am Here.

Love, Mumma

Opening

"Time for Thought of the Day meeting. Be there by 7:30 am!" Her roommate chirped like an alarm as she headed out the door.

Waking, She remembered where she was and latched onto her plan to leave today. *To where?* She had no idea yet, convincing herself that it didn't matter. She rolled over towards the open window – the scent of last night's rain still in the air – and noticed a ripped corner of the screen blowing in the wind. *See, this place isn't perfect*, She assured herself. The sheer white curtain moved slowly, curling around each damp whisper of wind. She had always been soothed by the presence of the wind, as something you couldn't see but knew was there with you. She imagined the wind whispering through the window. *I'm here with you.*

Judy appeared at her door, "Seems like you got a good night's sleep after all. I'll wait and walk you down to the 7:30 morning check-in group in the dining room." It rubbed her wrong. She dressed under Judy's watchful eye and grumpily followed her to the dining room where the smell of fresh coffee and blueberry pancakes foiled her plan to stay angry.

In the dining room, the morning light poured in. A woman spoke up. "HI, my name is Stephanie. I'm a grateful recovering addict and I hope everyone has a great day." *Unbelievable.*

Memories of her Mom, who was also named Stephanie, came fresh though. Then the comforting warmth of fresh-brewed coffee wafted throughout the room. She saw Big Sis across the table, who gave her a big friendly wave. Anger and warmth was all mixed up in that moment. Someone read from a book called *Each Day a New Beginning*. More alien concepts – like acceptance and forgiveness – bounced off the dining walls as women shared their fears and hopes for the day. Ashley came in a little late, pushing Kayla in a stroller. Judy had told her the babies weren't usually in group meetings and that the only people who interacted with them besides the mothers were volunteers. She really wanted to be mad about this intrusion, but Kayla *was* cute. Her innocent face touched her. For a moment, She felt happy that Ashley got to have her baby with her. She quickly noticed that Ashley was wearing the same sweatpants and ripped jacket she had worn yesterday. Maybe she didn't have other clothes. Or maybe she was too overwhelmed to take care of herself. Her thoughts went back to Emma. *If not today, I'll leave tomorrow.*

Later, She wandered to the backyard where everyone hung out and smoked, hoping to get the real deal on this place. There was some complaining about rules and gossip about someone's boyfriend hooking up with someone at a meeting, but mostly just joking around.

She overheard Big Sis telling an upset woman, "Take it to PDMA."

What the hell kind of cult is this? She wondered.

Judy yelled from the back porch, "Group Time," in this high-pitched voice as if she was inviting them to a party or something. She followed the stream of women back up the stairs. There, Judy informed her that her new counselor's name was Diana.

"Yikes, Diana's tough," She heard someone comment to some giggles behind her. Big Sis found her and told her she was heading to Diana's session herself.

She felt like a lemming walking towards a cliff, but followed Big Sis and a small group of other women downstairs to the basement where they would all meet with this Diana. The dimly-lit group room was tiny and smelled of… "Lemon?" I asked aloud.

"Diana uses essential oils in our group meeting and says lemon helps awaken and clear the mind," one of the women explained.

She slid into the group where eight women had gathered, sitting in a circle. She pushed her chair back in the corner, but was told by her new counselor Diana that She needed to sit in the circle in order to be part of the process. Diana spoke in a calm, firm voice as she assured her it was okay to just listen since it was her first PDMA. She wondered what the hell PDMA meant, but didn't care enough to ask.

Beth, a confident older woman who seemed to mistake herself for a staff member, read the group rules, "Keep confidentiality, equal air time, make I statements, give feedback based on personal experience, eyes must be open, no sugar coating, no swearing, and no name calling."

She took a moment to remind herself these rules didn't apply to her as she was not part of this cult.

Beth looked right at her and continued, "PDMA stands for Plan, Do Measure, Act. This is the most important group of the day where we open up and get uncomfortable." As if reading from a script, she said, "Out of our comfort zone is where the most growth happens."

Get uncomfortable? She thought. *Uncomfortable is all I know and all there is.*

Big Sis raised her hand and shared, "I didn't meet yesterday's goal of not calling my boyfriend; to be completely honest, when I called him he was high and lied to me about it."

"Do you want feedback?" Diana asked, instructing her to listen while other women gave feedback about their experiences with setting boundaries.

She didn't know anyone's name; but another one jumped right in, "The only person I can change is myself." Then another. "I was holding onto a reservation to relapse by calling people that are still in active addiction."

"What's in it for you to keep calling him?" Another one asked.

"I was afraid of being alone and eventually that took me out." Big Sis replied.

Two of the women said they would go with Big Sis to her phone time and help her reach her goal. Everyone seemed bossy. *Whose business is it anyways?* She thought. Big Sis thanked them for the support. *Support, is that what this is?*

She was relieved to just be listening till Diana looked at her and asked, "What's better?"

She stared right at Diana hoping she would leave her alone, but Diana held her calm demeanor like a pro, encouraging participation.

"What's better?" She finally reacted in a small voice. Her stomach tightened into a knot as Diana asked the question again, "What's better?"

She relented, "I have no money for cigarettes; my family is not speaking to me; I have nowhere to live; and my daughter is in state custody in a foster home with strangers. Nothing is better and nothing else matters!" Hot tears rolled down her cheeks amidst the thick silence in the room.

After a couple of minutes, Big Sis's voice eased into the awkward silence, "For me, it helps to think of one thing – big or small – that is better today because I am in recovery making better choices. Today, I didn't wake up sick or wonder what I did last night."

She heard her words but couldn't look up, surprised and embarrassed at her outburst. Diana closed the group with a moment of silence for those still suffering. Then she pulled her aside.

"I am looking forward to working together; you can and will recover if you do the work. Meet me in my office after lunch for your individual session," Diana offered.

She wondered what a session entailed, and silently assured herself she might be gone by then.

After the group, She ran into a long line of women waiting to get into the main office.

"Are you picking out of the basket today?" Her roommate Jen asked.

She had no idea what that meant and just stood frozen and confused, as usual.

Jen touted the rule, "If all roommates in a room make their bed and clean their room every morning for the whole week, we get to pick something out of Judy's prize basket."

She thought of how silly that was and then wondered what the prizes were. It was clear now why her other roommate Tina had told her to make the bed. When She saw Big Sis coming out of the office excited about a new makeup brush, her curiosity grew. But she hadn't made her bed that morning; pretty soon, she heard Tina grumbling about not getting a prize that week because the *new girl* didn't make her bed.

"Messy bed, messy head," She heard Judy telling someone who was arguing with her about having to make her bed.

She wondered why the staff worried about so many little details. *What's the big deal as long as we are not drinking and drugging?*

She stood in the foyer looking up at the winding staircase to the second and third floor. Everything felt like a maze, inside and out.

It seemed normal for the other women to go from group to group, like nobody else realized how pointless this all was. Seemed she was constantly on the move, going up and down the stairs, going from one meeting to the next. Walking down the long stairway to the backyard for another break outside, She wondered what the point of anything was.

"Up and down, up and down the stairs I go, all day long, for what?" She grumbled aloud.

Hearing the women in the group open up, ask for help, and support each other felt like landing on another planet. Her family didn't do that, her friends never talked like that, even the therapist her Mom sent her to – when she was a teenager – didn't talk to her about the real stuff. She saw a woman already sitting in the same tree spot she liked and decided to walk over anyway.

The woman said quietly, "Hi, I'm Sarah."

Sarah had a frail, disheveled way about her. Her matted hair stuck out from a dirty baseball cap and her blue sweatshirt seemed three sizes too big. It disarmed her. She found herself confiding in Sarah, "Pretty sure I am leaving today; this place isn't for me, but I'm not leaving to get high."

Sarah looked up with a haunted look, "I don't want to be here either. I left three months ago and didn't plan to get high either. But I did. I relapsed with my boyfriend. He overdosed and died."

Sarah seemed to look right through her. "I blame myself for his death. Maybe if I hadn't left treatment, he would still be alive today and our son would still have a father."

She didn't know what to say but couldn't walk away. She felt exposed and guilty. She didn't know why Sarah got so serious so quickly when they didn't know each other.

"I'm so sorry." She fumbled.

Sarah sat perfectly still, staring into the distance, as if looking for or waiting for something or someone. "Nobody ever thinks they are going to relapse when they run, but what are they really running to or away from?"

Everyone here seemed to be dealing with impossible things. In other programs, people didn't talk about the real things. They mostly gossiped and talked about how great the good old times were. This struck her as she looked at Sarah. Maybe this place wasn't all a joke; maybe these people weren't trying to fool themselves or someone else.

"Thanks for talking. I'm here … if you want to talk about anything." She offered awkwardly.

She went to her room, and started to write her autobiography. It wasn't too late for her; her daughter still had a mother.

Lying down after lunch, her mind relentlessly teetered on the fence of staying or leaving. She wondered who would even come pick her up. She thought about her sister Brenda. She missed Brenda but knew that Brenda would never pick her up. They used to be so close but Brenda had written her off after her second treatment. It was too much to think about. She dozed off, slightly induced by the mac and cheese lunch.

Big Sis woke her up with a message that Diana was waiting for her in her office in the annex. Half asleep, She wandered to Diana's office, mostly to avoid any suspicion about her potential departure plan. She eased into the comfortable yellow couch, the smell of lavender essential oil in the air.

In the calmest voice, Diana asked, "Tell me what brought you here?"

She deflected, "I really don't know how I am going to survive here with forty women."

Diana smiled, "Yes, it *is* overwhelming at first. Community living will be your greatest challenge at times and your greatest support. The connections you make with your peers will help you learn about yourself and build a strong recovery foundation."

"But there are so many women; how am I supposed to handle that?" She asked, wide-eyed, "I've never really gotten along with women; most of my friends are guys."

"You might all come from different backgrounds and experiences, but you have the common bond of addiction and how suffering affects your lives. As you all share pieces of yourselves, the magic and miracle of healing takes place. I know it is hard to imagine right now, but every woman you meet will touch your life. In some way – large or small – your pieces fit together. They become part of your community and help you build your recovery foundation. Things you may not be able to see in yourself, you will see in other women and relate to. You don't need to know all of the details or outcomes of someone's story to gain gratitude, perspective, or hope from meeting them." Diana explained, her eyes compassionate. "Now tell me what brought you here, to Everson," Diana asked, coming back to her original question, as if re-opening the door for her to walk through.

She suspected maybe this was some sort of trap to report her behavior to her social worker, but found herself opening up about losing custody of Emma.

"They just took her, ripped her right out of my arms." She continued. "I was trying to stop. Trying to do the right thing. I would never ever hurt Emma."

"That must have been really tough," Diana confirmed.

Diana really, really seemed to hear what She was saying. She felt like usually nobody ever heard her, saw her, without judging or misunderstanding her. It could have been the lavender, the comfy yellow couch, or Diana's gentle words that had her spilling out what felt like years of pain and confusion.

"How did this happen? Who chooses alcohol and drugs over their child? How do I ever fix this mess?" She asked, wearily to herself, shamefully to Diana. "My man and I were both drunk and fighting, as usual. Someone called the police and then they called social services when they realized we had a kid in the house, my little girl. My social worker had even warned me – one more incident and I would have to go to long term treatment."

Diana sat back in her chair, looked her in the eye, and asked, "What are your strengths?"

What a weird question, She thought.

"After all of that? Obviously, I don't have any strengths," She mumbled.

"Did you want to come to treatment; did you want to meet with me today?" Diana asked.

Unsure of whether to be honest, but feeling there was nothing to lose, She replied, "No."

"Could it be a sign of courage and resilience that you have made the difficult choice to come here in order to change and have a better life for you and Emma?" Diana asked.

The words spun around in her head, *Courage, Resilience, Choice, Better Life, Emma.*

Sensing her overwhelm, Diana offered, "I know it's all very intense right now; you've gotten yourself into a tough spot. I'll help you recognize your strengths and, from those strengths, you'll set daily goals. It will be challenging, but that's how you grow."

She nodded, trying to take it all in as Diana handed her a homework packet, "It's an honor getting to know you better. Get started on this written assignment and we will go over it next week. Oh, and let me know if you need a journal."

"I found my old journal and wrote in it last night," She replied, realizing it was the only connection she felt to her daughter right now. "It felt kind of soothing to write to Emma." She added, "It feels right to be writing again, even if only the few words I wrote last night."

She stood up to leave and Diana stood up too. Her soft brown hair framed her face nicely. Her face was kind. She could tell by the way she had listened and gently nodded that she had listened to many women like her at their darkest moments.

She retreated to the hall bathroom for a moment of solitude away from her roommates. While staring blankly at the wall for relief of some sort, the large soaking tub came into view. *How did I not notice this before?* She remembered soaking beneath steaming waters as a child every night after dinner. She became overwhelmingly homesick for a home. She had long ago sacrificed it for the thrill of recklessness disguised as independence. The tub was sparkling clean, as if nobody else had noticed it either behind the pink shower curtain. She turned on the faucet and climbed in as if getting away with something forbidden. The hot water seemed to seep into her broken parts, as if being wrapped in a favorite blanket. She became one with the velvet liquid – inside and out. She felt like water herself. She imagined the velvet-green stuffed turtle she used to have as a child swimming next to her. She soaked in the warmth and memories, drifting into its comfort. The cool night air breezed in through the tiny open window and smelled of distant crackling fire and logs. She longed for her old life prior to her spiral into addiction. Her weary mind pestered her. *How can you allow yourself a moment of relaxation or contentment when your life is so lost?* Another hushed voice overrode it, *Shhhhhhh* ... and she felt something opening inside her.

Dear Emma, I love you! It might not seem like it since you are with strangers, but please believe I love you! You would like this place where I am staying. It is a huge mansion three-stories high and forty women all live here together! There are a lot of friendly people here that really seem to care and the food is good. I had mac and cheese for lunch – your favorite! I took a bath tonight, or as you would say, tubbie. I am trying to get better and be the best Mom in the world because you deserve that. It's okay to get mad sometimes. I get mad but I am learning to talk about it and how to make better decisions. Also trying to figure out how to do it quickly so I can be home with you. Remember when we used to look out at the moon every night after reading Good Night Moon? Love you to the moon and back, Mumma

Unity

She decided to try a few days without a plan to leave.

The days were still long, one group after another.

She was afraid to talk about the things she had done. Others were somehow opening up, so it must be possible. She thought she knew what to expect from groups after almost a week and was happy not to be the newest one anymore. She saw other new women coming in which reminded her how impossible the first day had felt. Her first day seemed simultaneously a minute and a month ago.

She showed up for the afternoon group and everyone was already sitting in one big circle. She was nervous being face to face with everyone, all at once. The thought of being exposed was terrifying. After a meditation, eyes closed, they handed out chocolate. Chocolate always helps.

Anne, the Director, walked in, "Welcome to Unity Group where we talk about the importance of connection and community, focusing on similarities not differences. You have been given the gift of willingness and motivation to show up and do the challenging work of change here and now. Every challenge is an opportunity for growth."

Anne had excitement that made no sense. She talked like she was the one doing the things she was talking about. Her flowered skirt swayed and she talked with her hands like she was conducting an orchestra. Anne was tall and moved through the room with ease as she explained that the opposite of addiction was connection.

"Little by little, we are isolated by our addiction, removed from family, friends, and ourselves by the demand for escape. At first, it's an escape from reality, then it becomes an escape from the wreckage it causes," Anne explained.

She was distracted by Anne's shiny, pink high-heeled shoes, wondering why this woman cared so much. She looked around the room to see everyone listening intently. Something was happening here. She wasn't sure what, but it felt *different.*

Someone shared the definition of the word "unity" as a condition of harmony, parts that constituted a whole. While thinking of how silly this seemed, She realized she didn't feel the old familiar loneliness here that she had felt for so long, for her whole life.

Now, Anne was asking the women to give positive feedback to others who had made a change, and lift each other up. She was waiting for that uncomfortable silence to settle in over the group, but instead Big Sis called her out. She was surprised to hear Big Sis saying what "a power of example" she had been, making it through the first week and letting people support her. She felt embarrassed and could feel herself blushing, but the focus shifted as other women recognized changes in each other that inspired them to keep going when they had moments of hopelessness. These women seemed to really care about each other which made her slightly suspicious but not… angry. She looked across the room at Sarah, her hair still matted and her head bowed, and felt empathy for her, for the burden she was carrying. She wanted Sarah to have a better life and that small voice inside her whispered that she wanted the same thing for herself.

A girl named Becky commented, "The Unity Agreement this week was to *be the change you want to see.* It's been challenging. By focusing on *being* the change every day, I realized how much I actually sit back, blame other people, and wait for them to change. I wasn't even aware how much I romanticized my drug use until someone called me out. They called me a 'marshmallow.' This reminded me to stop glorifying my drug use and talking about it so much."

Cynicism crept in. She wondered why the hell anyone cared about this; people talked about drugs everywhere.

"Thank you for your honesty," Anne replied. "Awareness is a key component to change. If you aren't aware of an issue and you are not willing to be honest with yourself about it, you cannot begin to change it."

"I swear like a truck driver," Steph interjected. "Always have, always will, so what's the big deal?" She shrugged, "I know I'm new, but I don't see what the problem is."

No surprise, She thought, silently judging again. She observed Steph sitting on the edge of her seat, her ripped black jeans tucked into her combat boots, spiky short hair going in every direction, and apparently no clue that she stuck out like a sore thumb. Steph put no energy into trying to fit in, which She both hated and loved.

"Words have energy and power," Anne said calmly. "The words we choose and how we use them can build others up or tear them down. Does anyone have an example?"

Laura's hand shot up, "When I first got here, my social worker was at the house for a visit with my baby and she was considering whether to reunify my baby at the house. Two other women were in the dining room though talking and laughing about shooting dope, swearing, and being aggressive. My social worker reported this to her supervisor and they had second thoughts about placing my baby in the program here with me due to the possibility of an unsafe environment. Those two women may not have meant harm to anyone but their words caused a negative impression of the house."

Steph admitted, "I don't think I can break the habit of swearing and talking about the past."

Anne asked, "Do you talk to staff that way?"

Embarrassed, Steph replied, "Of course not," blushing while looking around.

"Oh, so you can pick and choose your words?" Anne asked through a smile.

She was surprised at how long this conversation went on and how much they cared about details here. Mom always said, *Little things make the big things*. Maybe there was something to that.

When it came time to pick a new Unity Agreement, Big Sis suggested, "Just do it, meaning don't overthink or procrastinate. Instead, jump into action. My friend Amy told me about this technique she saw on a video where you count 5, 4, 3, 2, 1 and then do the thing you need to do."

They took a vote and the daily check-in during PDMA for the unity agreement that week would be "Just Do It, 5, 4, 3, 2, 1."

The next morning, She woke up early, couldn't get back to sleep, and then went downstairs. Steph was up too and asked if She wanted to walk the Grace Trail with her. Big Sis had mentioned you could walk The Grace Trail between group meetings or during free time, but She didn't have a clue what that meant and didn't care to ask.

"Just do it," She laughed. So they walked across the driveway to a large rock with the words "Grace Trail" painted on them, colorful Fall leaves innocently sitting upon the letters.

"What does this trail mean?" She asked Steph.

Steph laughed, "No clue, it's just what we do here, I guess."

They decided to stop along the way at the other five rocks and figure out what they were. They came to the second large rock which had the word "Gratitude" painted on it alongside the question: *What are you grateful for?*

They looked at each other half-jokingly and blurted out, "Coffee" and "Smokes."

They laughed and kept walking. Then came the rock with the word "Release" alongside the question: *What do I need to release?*

One yelled, "Feeling guilty." Then the other yelled, "My anger at my Mom." The laughter this time was less than before.

Next, they came to a rock that had the word "Acceptance" painted on it with the question: *What do you need to accept?*

Looking at each other, one of them shouted out, "My boyfriend is a loser, and I'm in treatment." No laughter this time and they kept walking.

The "Challenge" rock was just around the corner with the question: *What is my next challenge?*

Steph quietly said, "Getting honest with myself, and finding a way to stay at Everson."

Silently, they walked to the last rock on the trail painted with the word "Embrace" alongside a question: *What can I embrace as possible?*

They turned towards each other, saying it nearly together, "Recovery!"

They walked the trail a few more times before going in for coffee, stopping silently at each rock.

"How was the Grace Trail this morning?" Judy asked as they walked up the front stairs.

"Nice," they replied, exchanging knowing smiles.

On Friday afternoon, everyone piled into the living room at 1:00 pm for "Graduation."

She had planned on trying to skip the afternoon group but was curious about graduation. She tried convincing herself that she didn't really care as she found a seat.

Five women sat on the main couch in the cramped living room. Everyone was so animated to see them. It sounded like they were all acting out a happy drama, but their expressions were so genuine. Anne thanked everyone for coming and explained that the first Friday of the month they honor the women that have completed the program over the past month. The women on the couch introduced themselves and seemed so proud and excited to be there. Becky was the first woman to speak while her baby was being passed around to other women, each one reaching for and cuddling the happy little girl.

"Hi sisters, I'm Becky, a grateful recovering addict."

It felt real, like Becky really was grateful. Her face was so transparent.

"Prior to coming to Everson, I was pregnant, unable to stop using and wanted to die. I arrived at Everson eight months pregnant, terrified, and alone. I was sure social services would take my baby when she was born. Then the miracle came. Because I was in treatment and working on myself, my baby was able to come home to Everson after a two-week detox."

Becky cried when talking about watching her baby detox and suffer because of her addiction.

"I never would have made it through the torturous process of forgiving myself if not for the support and safety of the women in the program, and my counselor Maria. I just sat in Maria's office and cried for the first month I was here, and then for the first month after the baby was born. I learned that I suffered from postpartum depression which I now know led to my relapse after my first daughter was born. If it weren't for the other Moms in the program, I never would have made it. They lifted me up when I was at my lowest, most desperate point."

Her daughter squealed with joy as one of the women tickled her.

"My one-year-old daughter Lilly is healthy, happy, and has a Mom, thanks to Everson. It's so important to open up and be honest with yourself, no matter how scary it is. All of the staff are here for one reason alone – to help you recover and restore your lives."

Becky giggled as she talked about the belly-aching laughs she'd had with the true friends she'd made at Everson. "I'll miss having coffee with my friends every morning."

"This is your one chance to get your life back, don't waste a minute." Someone encouraged her.

Everyone clapped as Becky choked back happy tears.

The four other women had similar stories to share and gave their own direct advice about putting everything into this once-in-a-lifetime opportunity.

"You didn't wake up addicted, sick, suicidal, or alone today, so thank your lucky stars," Andrea said with such conviction.

"Fact, life is still challenging and scary at times; but I have a strong support network and sisterhood with the women I went through the house with. I have found true joy, even amidst Life on life's terms. I am no longer chasing numbness through drugs, alcohol, drama, men, and old ideas of fun. Instead I have this peaceful excitement that life is good."

"It's nice to imagine that there is no finish line and that there is always more to learn. There is no such thing as perfect, and in recovery I do my best every day. I make mistakes every day, but I don't punish myself by picking up a substance," Andrea said.

The graduating women each thanked the staff for never giving up on them when everyone else in their lives had, including themselves.

One woman laughed, turning to the director, "Even when I lied to you and tried to manipulate everything and everyone, the staff calmly continued to help me look at my behaviors and how they were tied to my addiction. Nobody shamed me, and my healing was able to begin."

After each of the graduates spoke, some of the other women in the house stood up to thank them for coming and added a personal comment.

Big Sis jumped to her feet, "You all have such a beautiful light in your eyes; it gives me hope for my own recovery." Thanking them loudly for specific times they each helped her when she was struggling, Big Sis's loving nature shone through her gruff delivery.

Anne closed the meeting thanking the alumni, "This is what keeps the staff coming back during challenging times, being able to walk alongside you while you rekindle your will to live, finding your spark of life again. It's a blessing for each of us."

"Thank you for coming back to shine the light on the path for those who are sitting in this room unsure of how living with all of these women could ever help them recover. I offer the deepest gratitude and love to you all," Anne humbly concluded.

She sat slightly overwhelmed in the living room after all of the graduates and residents filed out of the room for strawberry shortcake in the dining room.

Becky came back and handed her a piece of cake piled high with whipped cream. "I know Judy would kill me for bringing food into the living room, but what the hell."

She took the cake while Becky did her best Judy imitation, "This house was here for you when you needed it and it has to be there for the women that need it after you, so take care of it."

They were both laughing when they realized Judy was standing in the doorway with her hands on her hips.

Becky shouted, "Love you Judy, you know imitation is the best form of flattery." She hugged Judy. "Judy, your voice is in my head every morning when I make my bed. Messy bed, messy head," Becky chimed, telling Judy that she should develop a Judy-voiced app for graduates for daily reminders to do the right thing.

She could not imagine how Becky could be so comfortable and happy, and wondered for a split second if she could ever be happy.

Dear Emma, I love you so much and can't wait to hug you again! I had strawberry shortcake today, you would have loved it. It was mostly whipped cream. I am sorry that things have been hard and we have been apart. Being your Mom has been the best part of my life. I made mistakes but will spend my life making it up to you. I need to see you soon but I'm afraid to reach out to social services. They said if I came to treatment they would arrange a visit, but I don't know if it was a trick. I'm slowly learning to talk to people and not be so afraid, but it's hard. I'm willing to do the hard work, no matter what, so I can be with you. Sometimes I still think about leaving and figuring it out myself. I know that's not a good idea, but I still fight it.

Love you to the moon and back, Mumma

Lost and Found

She woke up Saturday morning to the old, tired familiar debate in her mind: stay or leave. *The weekend seems like the perfect time to leave without too many staff to try talking you out of it*, the persistent voice gnawed at her. She didn't have a plan for where she would go or how she would get there but the old excitement of having a sneaky plan kind of felt good. Still, another part of her was starting to feel a little gross about quitting.

She would find a way to get to Emma somehow. She figured she would go to the Thought of the Day check-in to at least make it seem like she wasn't leaving.

The morning reading was about being in touch with feelings as a way to manage recovery. Apparently, how people *feel* about situations is why they relapse, not the situation itself. She wasn't sure how she *felt* and had never really thought about it. She closed her eyes and felt really lost. *Lost, is that a feeling?*

Big Sis opened the meeting, "I'm so anxious about the visit with my son today; he hasn't talked to me in three months. My son is my biggest motivation for recovery; but at the same time the guilt as a Mom is my biggest trigger."

Big Sis had always seemed so strong and it felt weird to see her tear up, her bottom lip quivering as she talked about how much she loved her 11-year-old son, Jordan, and how afraid she was that he would never forgive her. When Big Sis thanked everyone including her Little Sis for being there to support her, She felt a twinge of guilt for secretly planning to leave.

After breakfast they walked the Grace Trail for an hour as Big Sis laughed and cried while talking about her beloved son. “I'm so excited for you to meet Jordan this afternoon,” Big Sis said with a big bear hug.

Maybe I’ll leave later, Sunday perhaps, She thought.

Big Sis told her there was a note in “the duck” for her from Diana.

The duck, it just gets weirder, She thought. She went to the main office to retrieve her note and soon discovered why it was called the duck - a clothespin had been fashioned into a duck on the desk. The note was a reminder that – on Monday morning – Diana’s PDMA group would be going to the horse farm for equine therapy. She needed to be ready to leave at 10:00 am. She remembered someone saying they were going to the horses next week but hadn’t thought twice about what it meant. Then she remembered how her Grampy loved horses. She hadn't seen him in awhile, but he used to take her and her sister, Brenda, to the horse farm near the ice cream shop when she was little. Horses seemed like magical creatures when at the age of five. She wondered if they would still feel magical. The idea of going out on Monday and spending the day with the horses seemed better than trying to find a ride to who-knows-where on Sunday.

After the evening meeting, instead of following the stream of women heading out the front door to smoke, She went out the side door and sat alone under a beech tree. Looking up at the night sky She wondered why she was feeling melancholy. *What a strange word*, She thought, *one of those words whose meaning feels like it sounds. A vague, heavy sadness with no obvious reason.* She thought about seeing the horses tomorrow and it came flooding back to her. Brenda had disconnected from her during her addiction. It was easier to blame Brenda for being so angry, like it had nothing to do with her.

“What are you doing out here?” Big Sis asked, startling her as She gasped.

“Jesus, don’t sneak up on me like that. You scared the shit out of me.”

“Since when are you religious?” Big Sis giggled, “You okay?”

“Thinking about my sister,” She answered quietly.

“Your sister? I didn’t know you had a sister.”

“Sad, isn’t it? I have pretty much blocked her out. She hates me,” She mumbled.

"What's your sister like?" Big Sis asked.

She gazed back at the star-filled sky and smiled, "We have always been really different and used to fight a lot. I was sitting here remembering when we were young and would sleep over our Grampy's house. He would take us to the horse farm after dinner to feed them carrots. He would sneak them sugar cubes saying it was a special treat. Brenda and I would feed the horses through the fence and chase each other through the tall grass until it got dark. He would lie in the field with us telling us about the stars. Not sure if he really knew about astronomy or was making it up, but we loved it. We always got along when we were with Grampy; he knew how to just bring the silly out in us. I miss my sister and Grampy too."

She looked over at Big Sis who was looking up at the stars too.

"Thank you for always listening and really hearing me," She said.

Sunday morning brought a wild thunderstorm complete with torrential rain and wind. The sound of rain pounding on the window woke her up an hour before She had to be downstairs for Thought of the Day. The smell of rain crept through her open window and took her back to memories of making blanket forts on stormy days with her sister as a kid. There beneath the covers – where staff checked on you hourly – She felt safe. *But what about my plan to leave today on this perfectly stormy day?*

She drifted back to sleep and dreamt.

She was climbing a long winding staircase. The stairs were lined with carpet, then they became wooden like the backyard stairs. They seemed to lead into the clouds and she could hear her Dad's favorite song "Stairway to Heaven" playing. Emma was at the top of the stairs waving at her and she wanted to run to her, but her legs felt like they were disappearing beneath her.

Her alarm shocked her from the stairs back to her bed on this stormy Sunday. She felt beneath the covers for her legs and was relieved to find they were still there. She got up and raced to get to the Thought of the Day meeting. She bounced down the winding stairs, simply grateful to have legs, and to be there, to be found.

Dear Emma, I love you! It's hard and sad sometimes how much I miss you. I hope you are not too sad missing me. I am learning a lot here about how to be a better Mom. They teach us to wake up every day and start new instead of worrying about things and being stressed out. I will definitely be a better Mom and be able to play with you more and teach you things I am learning. We can do it together. Let's make blanket forts in the living room next rainy day when we are together. See you soon, I promise.

Love you to the moon and back, Mumma

Teddy

She had never looked forward to Monday mornings and getting back into the long weekday schedule, but today was different. She grabbed a thick sweater and pulled on the knee-high rubber boots Judy gave her from the horse farm bin. Skipping down the long staircase for morning coffee, She couldn't remember the last time she felt this excited. Judy yelled from the back porch for everyone from the group to meet in the living room.

Everyone was crammed into the living room when the program director Ann walked in asking, "What's the good news?"

She sat waiting for someone to crack a joke about good news. Being in rehab after all, some would say there is no good news.

Instead hands shot up. One by one, good news: *Another day sober, a wonderful family visit, getting a sponsor, and it's not raining today.*

She wanted to judge everyone for kissing ass, but instead found herself shouting out, "Going to the horses today." Like it was contagious.

Amanda raised her hand shyly, "How am I supposed to see any good news with all of the guilt and shame I feel?"

Anne asked them to check in on a scale of 1-10 with how much guilt/shame they felt. Most of the women shouted out, "8, 9, 10."

"Now close your eyes and come fully into this day, this moment," Anne suggested. "From the moment you got up this morning to this moment, how much guilt and shame have you created?"

Quietly people started saying, "0 and 1."

"That *is* recovery," Anne explained. "In recovery, people have a fresh chance every day to have a clean slate. They do not have to carry the weight of guilt day-to-day."

Diana followed up, "The process of recovery is facing the wreckage of the past without the burden of the past mistakes. It's living from an honest place that allows healing."

She felt the weightlessness of carrying no guilt for a moment; and for the first time ever, she felt the gratitude she had heard people talk about.

She gazed out the window from the backseat of the white minivan as Diana drove along leaf-carpeted roads to the horse farm. She could hear Diana giving instructions: no smoking, make sure to listen to the equine coach, and other things. She drifted back in time to Autumn's long past, her very favorite month. *Nature's letting go.* They arrived at Wheeler Farm at 10:00 am with journals in hand. She brought the journal she had been writing to Emma in, unsure of why they needed them; but sure Emma would not mind sharing with the horses.

The sweetness of the air caught her as She climbed out of the van. She remembered these smells from before: Hay, wood fire, manure, and sunshine. She smiled thinking about a horse farm- scented candle. A woman with dusty gray hair, knee high boots, and hay stuck to her flannel shirt came out from the barn introducing herself as the equine coach.

"Welcome, I'm Maggie and we're going to work with the horses and learn more about ourselves than some people do in a year's worth of therapy."

Maggie walked them to the edge of a fence where four horses were grazing in the field.

"Just be still and quiet and observe a horse, try and really connect."

She connected immediately with a large dark brown horse whose tail was gently swaying back and forth. Every now and then he would look over at her as he nibbled grass. She lost all track of time and the other women around her as She took in the majesty of the beautiful horse and the songs of the farm birds. For a moment, She wondered if these birds were extra happy because they were with the horses.

"Sit quietly and journal your observations," Maggie instructed.

She looked at her watch thinking ten minutes had gone by only to realize she had been observing the horse for over thirty minutes. She began to write about the horses' almost sacred presence, his strength, beauty, and the connection She felt. She wrote four pages, her hand aching. At one point She looked over to see Diana standing against the fence petting her brown horse and was so grateful for her. Diana had told them on the ride over that she rides horses. She was glad to have someone to talk to who understood the mysterious connections that happen with horses.

Maggie talked a lot about a horse's innate ability to be present and aware, explaining that horses are prey animals and they are always acutely aware of their surroundings. This also allows them to know when they are safe so they can relax.

"Our gut is our most intuitive part of our bodies and horses are all gut, thus ultra-intuitive with their surroundings, including people they are around. The connections we just made," Maggie clarified, "are true connections, true presence, truth."

She loved the idea of *truth* for some reason and wrote about it in her journal as Maggie was talking. Truth seems to be what *is* in the moment you are in. It connects to what She felt this morning in group, that by being present in this one moment there is no actual guilt or shame. Stillness seemed to have a way to bring truth to the surface. She thought about this, standing quietly and just *being* with the horse for a half hour.

"The horse you observed will be the horse you work with today," Maggie announced.

As they stood up, She locked eyes with her brown horse.

"That's Teddy," Maggie said, introducing her formally to majestic Teddy. His shiny brown coat drew her in, like She was looking into him.

"Stand right next to Teddy, observe his behavior and get a feel for his personality. You are also letting him get a feel for you." Maggie guided.

She felt overwhelmed by the horse's might up close, yet at the same time sensed his gentle nature. He looked her in the eye for what seemed a long time and She quietly began to tear up. She didn't feel sad, she just *felt a* lot. It was like Teddy knew her better than She knew herself without words.

"Keep your arms by your side and stay truly present and open."

She hoped she would be able to reach out and touch Teddy soon. Did he feel as soft as he looked?

"Moving to the inside pen," Maggie said so matter-of-factly it broke the spell for a moment.

As they were walking, a huge gray horse was being hosed down on the side of the building and suddenly he broke loose. The gray horse seemed aggravated and came running towards the group of women. Teddy was behind the fence but came running alongside the fence near the group, seeming very concerned. Teddy came up alongside the fence right near the bucking gray horse, neighing loudly as if to tell him to calm down. The gray horse slowed his march and calmed down. She was certain that Teddy had come to their rescue with the aggravated horse. When they got into the indoor arena Maggie told them they would be going into the ring with the horse. Trish said that she had a scary experience with a horse when she was a child and was terrified, even though she felt a strong connection to her horse Mable.

She volunteered to go first and approached Teddy who was standing in the back corner of the ring.

Maggie remained outside of the ring saying, "Walk slowly towards the horse."

As She got closer she could feel his presence getting stronger.

"Approach Teddy from the left side so he can fully see you and not be scared," Maggie instructed.

"Extend your arm, offering the back of your hand to his nose. This is the horseman's handshake where he acknowledges your presence and accepts your touch."

Teddy's nose was warm against her skin and his eyes were an even deeper brown than his coat.

"Thank you for accepting me, Teddy," She whispered.

His fur was as velvety and luxurious as it looked and he smelled of earth, strong and rich. Maggie told her to walk around the horse slowly. When She got to the back-right side of the horse she was overcome by how powerful this creature was. She sensed that his power was so strong that it could have been scary, but all she could feel was his love and grace. Teddy was breathtaking.

After walking around Teddy, Maggie instructed her to come out of the ring.

"When I observed you getting to the back-right side of the horse, even as a coach, I sensed the connection you have with Teddy."

Trish went into the ring with the horse and stood still. Her horse Mable slowly approached her and laid his head on her belly. He stood alongside her with his head on her swollen belly. She wondered if it was possible that the horse could tell that Trish had liver disease. Was Mable sensing this? Trish smiled gently, knowing she picked the right horse.

Later, they sat outside the barn in the field eating their bologna sandwiches. She hadn't had bologna since she was a kid. This strange field trip was just what She needed. It was nice having a break from debating with herself about leaving Everson. The air carried the scents of earlier – hay, sunshine, and water with the earthy twinge of manure. She watched as Trish took a deep breath with her eyes closed and hoped she felt as peaceful as she looked.

After lunch they went back into the indoor ring and were told they would be working with their particular horse and learning to pick up its back leg. She had seen this in a movie and felt slightly nervous, but felt that Teddy had trusted her and knew that she trusted him. She placed her hand on his hindquarter and ran her other hand down his leg just as Maggie had instructed. When She got to Teddy's ankle he had not begun to pick up his foot, so she gently squeezed the back of his leg, still nothing.

She looked to Maggie who said, "Set an intention to help Teddy lift his leg, not to control the situation."

She didn't think She was trying to control anything; but let go of her annoyance, closed her eyes, and simplified her intention, not her plan. Teddy worked with her and lifted his strong smooth leg with ease. She felt gratitude to him and then felt her words come easily, "I love you."

On the ride home Diana asked a simple, "How was it?"

A few of the women laughed realizing they had not even thought about having a smoke break the entire day.

"The horses must be magic." Jen giggled. Trish asked if they were going to be able to go back to the horse farm next week. She sat soaking it all in hoping the magic would stick with her well beyond Teddy's indoor ring.

Dear Emma, I love you! I made a new friend today, a beautiful brown horse named Teddy. It reminded me of how Grampy and I would stop at the horse farm after taking you for ice cream and you would talk to the neigh-neigh's. I feel good today, like I know what hope is. I hope and pray that you feel good too. I am learning that maybe I do not need to punish myself for making mistakes and start looking at what I am doing right. I am going to work on seeing you soon.

Love you to the moon and back, Mumma

Layers

Diana asked if She would like to contact her family about scheduling a family meeting. She declined, convinced they still wanted nothing to do with her due to losing custody of Emma to social services. Her Mom had said she was *not able* to take custody due to her work schedule and She had not forgiven her for that. How could her Mom let them send her only granddaughter to a stranger's house? On some level She knew it was not her mothers' fault but she needed someone else to blame besides herself. Taking the blame fully felt like it would kill her one way or another. She knew she still had parts of what happened the night Emma was taken locked away in her mind and needed to keep it that way to survive. When Emma was born She loved her so perfectly and swore she would always be there to take care of her. But She was not there. There was nobody else to blame anymore. It had been her choice all along.

Becoming a Mom was strange for her. She never thought she wanted to have children because of what she saw her parents go through with her and her sister. It just seemed hard and She didn't see the benefit. She had been very insecure in the relationship with her boyfriend and was happy when she got pregnant, thinking it would make their relationships stronger. She convinced herself that it made them closer but in reality, it just made her try harder and it just made him still pull away. She did all of the work for both of them, not drinking during the pregnancy while he continued to party, working two jobs while he worked part time, finding them an apartment, and accepting his mean comments about her family. Even back then She hung on for the fantasy of a happy family where she would feel safe and loved. She could not imagine what made her think this was possible with Josh, except for blind wishful thinking. She had never really felt safe or known what that feeling was. *Are you supposed to know what safe feels like?* She wondered.

She felt like he knew what she didn't want in her new little family – not an angry alcoholic father and a mother who covered everything up and pretended. Yet, that *is* what She had created. She feared to admit it. She never could figure out how to fix things, so She had given up on some level and chosen to numb it all out.

She was sensing now, little by little, that there was another way to live; other women were doing it and made it seem possible. With two parents with addiction issues, Emma was going to need guidance and love more than ever. She knew without a doubt she wanted to be the one raising her daughter, taking her to the playground, helping her make different choices, and truly breaking the family cycle. Long buried grief, anger, sadness and confusion from her Dad's passing began to surface. She quickly shoved it back, way back to the darkest corners. *How is it that her Mom didn't save him? How did I not save him*?

The group counselor, Bethany, told her to write a timeline of her life. It was called "Building History." She had three days to get it done. Bouts of feeling clearer, better, and less angry continually mixed with wanting to give up on herself all together. *Isn't it enough that I have to live this nightmare?* She thought. *Now they want to torture me and have me write it down?* Convinced She couldn't do it, she took the timeline assignment and plopped down. Other women were sharing different assignments which seemed impossible as well. There they were literally reading out loud the various damages their addiction had caused them: relationship damages, physical damages, emotional damages, opportunity damages, moral damages, and more. Basically, writing about a typical day in addiction.

"This is insanity for real; what can be the point of this?" She mumbled, punishment is all she could think of.

"Do you have a question?" Bethany asked.

She shrugged, "Why?"

Bethany continued, "Would anyone in the group be willing to share how doing this Building History assignment has helped them?"

Jean shared, "I had convinced myself that my addiction didn't really impact my life or my relationships until I started doing the assignments and realized how it truly affects all areas of my life."

Debbie shared, "I have been through at least a dozen other programs and never looked at the reality of my active addiction, so I just kept repeating it until now. Having to take an honest inventory of the impact my alcoholism has had on my family, job, and health – every part of my life – has helped me make a lasting decision for recovery."

Jess shared, "I was terrified coming into this group the first day, but when women started reading their assignments I felt connected to them and realized I was not alone. That I was not the only one who had done unspeakable things."

"Think about it this way," Bethany suggested. "If the woman sitting next to you has been through similar things and you believe she deserves a better life, maybe you deserve a better life too."

Three days later, She read her timeline in the Building History group. It felt good and clean somehow reading it all out loud. The timeline ended with her coming to Everson and She felt a twinge of pride that She did the right, the hard thing. Bethany asked her to bring the timeline to her session with Diana and look for the patterns. Patterns with addiction and relationships and other self-destructive behaviors that often accompanied substance use. The group was not a feedback group which made it easier, She thought. *Speak the truth and move on.*

When She was done reading, Bethany said "Thank you and good job" and they moved on to someone else.

She was left with her own sense that she had no idea who she was without these self-destructive patterns. As grateful as She was for her daughter, she kind of envied the women who didn't have children due to the enormous weight of guilt attached to being a Mom and hurting her daughter. Late at night, She often tormented herself with the reality that her love for her daughter had not been enough to overcome her own destruction and self-punishment. The minute Emma was born She felt a love so strong she could have never imagined. She was sure this love would sustain her beyond her addiction. This dreaded guilt had long been the fuel for her relapses, unable to face the reality of her rampant addiction. Now there was a sliver of hope – and even relief – from watching other women share their stories.

"You can use your timeline for an outline for your autobiography," Bethany said.

She had put down her autobiography assignment when she got to her dad dying.

Her roommate Jen shared, "Finishing my autobiography eased my fear of the past. When I finished it, there it was – in black and white – and the place hadn't fallen down around me and I hadn't imploded."

Jen seemed to have a perspective She wanted, so she made a commitment to finish her autobiography by the end of the week. On Friday, She handed her finished autobiography to Diana. It felt good, like closing a dark chapter. She did not include the details of her dad dying. She still had no words.

Dear Emma, I miss you, miss you, miss you, that's it! I am going to face my fears and contact the social worker today so that I can see you. I have finally realized that I need to get better, and do it here so that we never have to be apart again. I am working really hard. Seems there is no easy way to the other side of tough things, but I will be here to teach you all of this my little peanut butter and jelly sandwich girl. I think of you drawing pictures for me every night as I write to you and it helps me feel connected to you.

Love you to the moon and back and back again, Mumma

Outside World

Having completed her autobiography, She earned the privilege of using her cell phone for an hour and a half a day.

Judy called to her after lunch, "We are going to clean out your phone."

This made no sense to her.

While people wandered in and out of the main office, Judy sat asking about the contents of her phone, contacts, text messages, and pictures that needed to be deleted because they were not supportive of recovery and could trigger her.

Who does this woman think she is? She thought, then said, "There's nothing that needs to be deleted."

They began looking through the contact list together and right there in black in white was her drug dealer, ex-boyfriend, someone named slut, another *friend* named dope, and countless other random people who would no doubt *discourage* her recovery. She felt embarrassed as they combed over and deleted contacts and pictures of her high and drunk – all of this mixed in with pictures of beautiful, sweetest Emma.

Shame screamed in her face as she reread horrible text fights with her boyfriend who called her garbage and other awful names.

She was wrung out from the reality of the life she had accepted – a sad walk down a difficult memory lane. Judy seemed to be matter-of-fact about witnessing the train wreck life that her phone revealed, like it was just another Friday afternoon.

Of course, this woman is being paid to do this, she must be a professional faker.

At the moment of her renewed hopelessness, She looked up at Judy who said with a smile, "No worries, you are starting a new life with new friends that will support you no matter what."

She sees me, She thought, a*nd didn't kick me to the curb or throw me away*.

"All cleaned out," Judy said, releasing her momentarily from the land mines of shame.

She didn't dare reach out to her family since she had not spoken to her mother or sister in almost six months. She didn't have any supportive friends, so she listened to her favorite music for an hour and almost felt normal.

She looked at Facebook and saw her ex-boyfriend and father of Emma, Josh, partying with another woman. She felt an overwhelming urge to leave and find him, to tell him how he had hurt her and how he had no right being happy. Deeper than anger was the hurt She felt that they were no longer together. Didn't he want to be a happy little family with Emma? Wouldn't he clean up his act for his daughter that he claimed to love, but never saw?

*Wait, fuck all of tha*t, She thought. *I have made mistakes too. Maybe we can get back together and help each other stay sober. For Emma of course.* It all made perfect sense. She was starting to get better and could really help him. She messaged him, waiting anxiously for his response. He didn't respond; she started spiraling and convinced herself that he would come pick her up and start their new life together. Even though he was almost ten years older than She was, she could show him the way.

5:00 pm came and it was time to turn her phone in but Josh still hadn't responded to her message yet. Staff came looking for her to turn her phone in. Panic struck. All She could think about was how to get access to her cell phone which was locked in the staff office closet.

"My mother had surgery today and I need to call and check on her," She anxiously told Shirley the Recovery Aid in the main office, her stomach churning within the lie.

Shirley checked the communication log, "Sorry, your counselor didn't leave a note about you using your phone. If it is an emergency I can let you use the staff office phone."

She would not be able to *get to* her phone. She felt caged and trapped. The last time She felt this way was when she couldn't get in touch with the drug dealer.

"Snack time," her roommate chirped, "Why do you look so sick?"

The word struck her between the eyes. She was sick. She felt sick and now other people could see it.

For the first time in a long time She felt hungover the next day, emotionally wrung out. After freaking out about Josh, lying to staff and basically getting caught, and then obsessing all night about what was wrong with her that he didn't want to be with her, She was drained and uneasy. In her head, She knew he was a bad guy; but maybe that was because he was sick too, and if he could get better they could be okay, together. She didn't want to be one of those pathetic women that needed a guy to be okay. This was different; they had Emma together and if that was enough for her to get better maybe it would be enough for Josh too. She wanted to talk to someone but didn't want a lecture. The softer voice inside her spoke again, telling her something felt gross about wanting things so much with Josh when she knew things had been horrible in their relationship.

In the PDMA group, Diana asked, "What's better?"

She forced herself to say, "I'm not with Josh."

It felt like She was stepping into reality in some small scary way. She felt a sense of safety in the truth.

That night another girl, Patty, shared how much more relaxed she felt from doing acupuncture.

"Isn't that the thing where they poke you with needles?" She asked her.

"You can't even feel it," Patty insisted. "As soon as they put the first tiny needle in your ear you feel an overall sense of calm, then we listen to a guided meditation. Plus, we get to get out of here and go downtown to RWW, a program that helps women in recovery."

Going for a ride anywhere was a sell for sure. Judy put acupuncture on her list and the next Tuesday, She piled into the van with Diana and the group heading to downtown.

"Welcome to Recovery Without Walls. I'm Bill!" The man cheered, like they were celebrities. "Thanks for joining us!"

Super weird that you'd thank us, but whatever floats your boat, She thought. But Bill's undeniable Irish charm shined through his blue eyes and the wispy gray hair combed back from his classic forehead. As he welcomed them in, She softened a bit, as he reminded her a little of Grampy and made her want to see him again soon.

She didn't remember much after sinking back into the zero-gravity chair, getting under a warm blanket, and the acupuncturist gently put the first tiny needle in her ear.

"We are going to raise and connect our vibration through chanting *Om* together," Arla the acupuncturist invited in the most soothing tone.

She lost count of how many times they chanted, mesmerized by their united field of sound. The guided meditation started and She drifted off, to somewhere far away, yet deep within. A warmth moved through her body – and seemingly through her spirit – as She was guided to become fluid, like water, and release, simply release. She felt everything starting to fall away, sadness, fear, uncertainty, doubt, addiction, recovery, family, and finally, her old self. As Arla took the last needle out She came back from her happiest place. She looked around the room where Diana and the other five women were sitting. Something was different, like something had been removed from her. She couldn't tell what it was, but it felt real.

On the way out Bill replied, "Keep coming and don't drink; it's worked for me for 35 years!"

She enjoyed the ride in the van back to the house as if a little child going to the park. She felt younger, lighter. They drove by the beach and Diana said staff would be taking them on a walk to the ocean during the 1:00 pm group today. She thought about the cheery man at RWW and asked Diana about him.

Diana explained, "Bill started Recovery Without Walls over 15 years ago to support women in recovery bridge the gaps and challenges that pull them off course. Everson Program Director Anne and Bill both have a deep commitment to finding ways to help women heal and remain in long-term recovery. Everson and RWW have been partnering on this mission for years.

"That's awesome," She replied. She could not fathom how yesterday felt like the worst day ever and today the best. When She had been out there drinking and using – running from everything – every day was the worst day.

The walk to the beach was a meditative walk so they were not allowed to talk to anyone until they got to the beach a half mile away. The burnt orange and red leaves that had been swaying in the wind outside her bedroom window were now strewn about the sidewalk. As much as She loved Autumn, she had always felt sad once the leaves finally fell. The brightly yellow, orange, and red colored sidewalks called to her spirit with the beauty of letting go, being in the flow of change. When they got to the bridge, She looked out over the harbor and swore a dolphin poked its nose up out of the water. She wanted to yell for everyone to look but just enjoyed the private visit all to herself.

When they got to the beach She took off her sneakers and wiggled her bare feet in the sand. She felt grounded and calm as she looked out over the vast ocean. She breathed in the salt air and realized the anxiety she had carried for as long as she could remember was gone. She wasn't beating herself up about the past or worrying about the future. She wasn't craving an escape, or pacing back and forth inside of herself like a caged animal. *Could it really have been the effect of acupuncture?* She didn't want to think or question it anymore. She just wanted to enjoy the beach.

When they got back to the house Diana told her that She had received a call from her mother asking how she was doing. She was afraid to face her mother's disappointment and didn't want to return her call alone. Diana suggested they make the call together on speaker phone for additional support for the first call.

"Maybe tomorrow," She suggested.

"I'm not in tomorrow," Diana replied. "I know your Mom is available this afternoon; let's call."

In the spirit of good old' *discomfort*, She agreed and they called her mother.

"I know apologies mean nothing at this point, and I have to prove I'm serious about getting better," She managed to blurt out when her mother said hello.

Without allowing a response from her mother, She continued, driven by fear of what her mother would say to her. “This place is different from the rest; people actually get better here.”

“Have you seen Emma?” Mom asked calmly.

She choked up at the mention of her daughter's name. She felt like she needed to keep those feelings locked up, private between herself and Emma in her journal. She feared she didn’t have the strength to face her social worker and the ugly reality of losing custody. This was mixed with anger at her mother for not taking custody of Emma.

“I’m sorry. I can’t talk anymore. I’m sorry.” She said, embarrassed and panicked.

She hung up with her mother, left Diana’s office, and wept in the backyard, her heart broken open. She had avoided the women in the program who had their babies with them, afraid if she talked about Emma the distance between them would all be more real somehow. Debbie brought her son Jason to the backyard and handed him to her. She knew Debbie had lost permanent custody of her other son Jacob, yet saw the deep love in Debbie’s eyes and welcomed Jason into her arms. An overwhelming wave of grief, love, loss, hope, and acceptance washed over her as She faced her deepest fear. That afternoon She contacted her social worker to ask about visitation with Emma.

After lunch She was called to the main office, and slightly panicked wondering if She had done something wrong, checking the corners of her mind. Was it the snack She had brought to her room or was it spending too much time on the payphone last night?

As She entered the office, Judy said, “Good news! We’re moving you out of the triple room, into a double room on the third floor. We’ve all noticed how hard you are working to make progress on your goals.”

She was taken off guard by the good news and was oddly unsure if She wanted to move. Surely a double room on the third floor was a step up.

“Can I think about it?” She asked.

Judy encouraged, “You need to set an example in the house for new women. Only responsible women can move to the third floor.”

She felt resistance at the thought of rooming with someone new. Her two roommates could be annoying at times, but at least they were used to each other. Now She was told she *needed to move*, a switch from *getting to move*. She understood but kind of enjoyed the feeling of resistance and wanted to rebel. She didn't need another pep talk about change and how *getting comfortable with being uncomfortable was how growth works.* She thought of how her young daughter stomped her feet and marched around when she was angry, and wanted to do the same thing. Instead, She quietly thanked the staff and walked out of the office. She snuck upstairs to Room 32 to see the new room, hoping she would hate it and have a second chance at rebelling. Standing along the circular wall of large windows though, She could see the ocean off in the distance, blue water gently moving back and forth.

"Beautiful," She whispered, drifting back to playing on the beach with her daughter as the waves gently splashed on the beach. Memories that up until this moment had been too painful to allow.

Dear Emma, I Love You! I walked to the beach and walked barefoot in the sand. As soon as I can, I will take you to the beach and we will build sandcastles. Life seems simpler now; sorry I was distracted a lot and did not play with you enough. The most important thing to me is being there and playing with you. I talked to Nana today; she is still mad at me I think. I was afraid to talk to her. I am sorry I have hurt everyone with my choices. I moved to a new room today in the big house I am staying at, maybe when you visit you can see my room. I am sure I will see you soon! Love you to the moon and back, my sweet peanut, Mumma

Disease

Through the daily routine and structure, She began to build confidence in herself. Her commitment to getting better was growing. She now looked forward to an upcoming visit with Emma.

She had become a "Big Sis" to Jamie, a newcomer. Once, She had overheard Jamie talking on the payphone about getting something dropped off near the dumpster in the backyard. She was worried that Jamie was trying to sneak drugs or alcohol into the house and was unsure of what to do. Jamie had a shifty, uneasy way about her, always whispering to other women and looking around to see if staff was around. She wanted to let staff know but didn't want to be known as a rat. She convinced herself that it was none of her business. Later that night Jamie was acting strange. She figured it was none of her business and in some small old familiar way wondered what Jamie used and if she had anymore. She finally confided her concerns in Big Sis who went directly to the staff. Staff assessed Jamie and immediately transferred her to the detox facility for medical attention and safety.

RA staff member, Tina, held a meeting with everyone to reinforce how they needed to speak up if they saw or heard something unsafe. Tina was young, but confident and super direct. You could tell Tina had been through some rough things in her own life and wasn't going to take crap from anyone. Her long brown ponytail swayed back and forth as she stood in the doorway shifting from side to side.

"By withholding information about another person getting high in the house, you are risking relapse yourself due to the sneaky insidious nature of this disease," Tina stated.

Lying in bed that night, She asked her new roommate Jen, "What did you think about what Tina said?"

"I don't see the big deal; but when I noticed Jamie was high, I'll admit I kind of wanted to get high too and didn't say anything," Jen admitted.

"I thought about searching Jamie's room after she left. But I realized I actually don't want to get high anymore and live that life," She murmured.

As She was saying her prayers that night she prayed to have the clarity to see *the disease* as if it was in front of her, or as if it were sneaking up on her again. She said a prayer for Jamie and for Big Sis for doing the right thing.

During the Thought of the Day check-in group the next morning, people were angry, sad, confused and shocked that Jamie had brought drugs into the house. There were suspicions that other people got high with her. The tension could be cut with a knife. It seemed like people wanted someone else to blame besides Jamie, saying staff should have known and that they had better let her return to the program. She felt guilty that she didn't say anything when she heard Jamie on the phone and didn't tell the staff.

At 9 am instead of the PDMA group, the director Anne called a meeting with everyone in the living room about the importance of speaking up and standing up for the safety of their environment.

"When you leave this program you will be confronted with situations in which remaining in recovery depends on your ability to speak up for yourself."

"Close your eyes and think back to the situation that brought you into treatment, the specific event, hitting bottom," Anne instructed.

"I want you to share that situation in one sentence with no fluff or excuses." The conviction and intent in Anne's voice rippled out into the room.

A woman named Sarah shared, "I was in recovery, but I relapsed and woke up next to my boyfriend who had died of an overdose while I slept next to him."

One by one, other women shared.

"I woke up after a blackout and didn't know where my kids were," Tara gulped.

"I took a handful of pills and was angry when I woke up because I could not live dope sick anymore," Lisa admitted.

"I was arrested for prostitution because it was the only way I could get money for drugs," Nina cried.

"I woke up so sick from drinking that I had to drink first thing in the morning to stop the shakes or I couldn't feed my baby," Pam shared.

She finally faced her truth, "The police removed my daughter during a drunken argument with my boyfriend, and I lost custody." The words spilled onto the floor like shattered glass.

The pain of every woman in that room was palpable.

Anne asked, "Raise your hand if you want to go back to this moment."

Nobody raised their hands.

"How many people believe if you were to pick up a drink or drug again this is where you will return to?" Anne continued.

Every hand raised.

"Who is willing to speak up and stand up for their recovery today?"

Every hand shot high into the air.

During their individual session later, Diana asked her, "Let's circle back to something we discussed during your intake."

She was nervous about what that could be, a few weeks seemed so long ago and she couldn't remember most of what they talked about.

"Tell me more about the anxiety you reported having as a child," Diana asked.

"When I was the age of five, my mother took me to the doctor because of my ongoing stomach aches."

She thought for a while, as Diana allowed the usual silence which now felt comforting and not torturous. "I don't remember much of my childhood, but I do remember sitting on the crinkly white paper on the table in the doctor's office while the doctor told my mother, *It's all in her head*; *She's fine.*

She didn't wait for Diana to ask how that felt.

"I didn't understand that because my stomach rolled around doing somersaults every morning before school. From that morning on, my Mom would mimic the doctor as she pushed me onto the bus stairs saying, *You're okay, it's all in your head.* Maybe that's when I realized there was something wrong with me." She said quietly, sinking back into the yellow couch.

"Do you believe there is something wrong with you?" Diana asked.

She sifted through the question feeling like there *must* be something wrong with her. *I'm in rehab.*

She looked up at Diana timidly, "No, there was and is nothing *wrong* with me but I did need help," remembering how that five-year-old girl felt, and imagining Emma.

Nodding knowingly, Diana said, "It sounds like anxiety; how long have you suffered with it?"

She was struck by the word suffered, nobody had ever understood how she felt. Thinking back, She realized that when she started drinking with the neighborhood kids at the age of thirteen, her anxiety went away.

"When I picked up my first drink. It went away. I could be in my body and not feel like something was *wrong*, like I was *wrong*. It just all went away and I knew I had found a way to survive."

She had never connected the dots before.

"Sounds like you were self-medicating, "Diana commented.

"Of course, and it worked!" She exclaimed, feeling astonished at how the pieces fit.

As they explored the layers of her anxiety She realized how she went from anxiety, to alcohol, to drugs when alcohol got sloppy. Landing her smack dab in the middle of denial and anger. She shuddered at the thought of letting go of these protective yet unhealthy *coping skills*, as Diana called them.

"What now?" She was scared, that was it. What if all of this work and struggle to change only worked while She was at Everson? During addiction education class they taught about the nature of addiction being a *chronic disease*. At first, She felt relieved it wasn't her fault that she had this *disease.* Then She felt hopeless that she would have to fight it every day for the rest of her life. There were women in the house that had been there before, who had done all of the work and still relapsed and come back. She knew she was afraid of getting her hopes up, building this better life in recovery, only to go back down the tubes.

After dinner, She was sitting on the back porch alone when Laura, a Recovery Aid, asked her, “What’s so serious?”

She took a chance, “I am afraid of doing all of this work, then losing it all.”

Instead of dispensing words of wisdom, Laura simply asked, “Are you in recovery today?”

“Of course I am, but I am here,” She answered, slightly annoyed, not wanting a crusty old slogan. She wanted to be reassured that this would work.

“Being in treatment does not guarantee you are in recovery,” Laura calmly replied. “It’s the actions you take today and the decisions you make that define your recovery. It is possible to continue the same healthy habits when you leave and remain in recovery long-term.” Laura continued, “I went through Everson five years ago and thought I had it all figured out. I eventually stopped going to meetings when work got hectic, stopped talking to my sponsor, and eventually thought I could drink normally. I was right back at rock bottom within two weeks.”

“Then what? “She asked, overwhelmed by it all.

“I made it back to treatment, dug deeper, and now I do the things that support my recovery every day.”

She mumbled, “That sounds like a prison sentence.”

Laura shrugged saying, “It’s pretty simple. I hit a morning meeting, pray to stay away from a drink or drug, talk to my sponsor a few days a week, help the newcomer, and I have a good life. I tried to stop drinking for years and couldn’t, that’s my version of *prison.*” Laura paused before continuing, “It’s kind of like being diabetic. You take your medicine every day by doing what works, then get on with your life.”

She had a sense that she was actually *getting on with her life* and, in that moment, gave herself permission to be a little bit afraid but to hope.

A young woman named Alex was back, after having completed the program a year ago. She was curious and asked Alex what happened to bring her back.

"I knew the first time I was here that there were things I was not willing to talk about or face, and those things waited for me and took me back out even lower than I imagined. I had felt oddly *safe* with my secrets before, but they really do keep you sick. Make sure and leave no stone unturned when doing your assignments," Alex warned.

In group, they were assigned a Relationship Damage Assignment. She started filling in the blanks of stealing from her grandmother, blowing off her Mom's birthday party because she couldn't get a hold of the drug dealer, letting Emma cry endlessly because she was too drunk to make a bottle, and countless other acts of destructive selfishness. She didn't recognize the woman she was writing about.

Today, She got up on time, made her bed, said her prayers, brushed her teeth, ate breakfast, helped other women stay when they wanted to leave, did her chores, and didn't hurt anyone. In recovery, She knew how to make the right choice and when she did make mistakes, it was no big deal. She didn't need to lie every day all day in order to keep fooling herself.

On the way to the smoke pit, She noticed a stone on the side of the walkway engraved with the word "Believe," propped beside a small angel statue. None of the women in the backyard knew what the stone represented but assured her that Judy would know. She saw Judy walking to the annex building and asked her about the stone.

Judy told her about a young girl named Alish who was at Everson years ago, "She completed almost three months and went home on an overnight pass for an appointment three days before graduation from Everson. Alish snuck out to visit her ex-boyfriend while home. He was abusive to her, as he always had been. Alish ended up using heroin *one last time,* overdosed, and died in her sleep on her parents' couch. When we packed up her room we found thank you letters she had written to all of the staff, talking about how excited she was to have her life back."

Judy quietly remembered aloud the day Alish's family came to Everson and asked to talk to the women in the house. Her mother had pleaded with them to value their lives and had reminded them that one last time could be *the* last time. With tears in her eyes, Alish's Mom thanked the staff for giving them their daughter back for the last three months.

"You could feel that part of her heart and soul had died when Alish left this world," Judy shared. "Her family donated the angel statue and the Believe rock as a memorial to Alish. I say a prayer every time I walk by it."

She asked if Judy would share that story at the next house meeting, knowing that it touched her deeply and that everyone could use a connection to this Everson Angel.

Dear Emma, You are an Angel; I know you are. You were sent here to save me. I am in class all day learning about why I made the poor choices I made. Up until recently I had convinced myself that I was a bad person for repeatedly making choices that I knew were going to mess up my life. I began thinking I was hopeless which hurt so much because I love you and want to be my best for you. I didn't know how; I didn't know that there were scientific medical reasons that I reacted to alcohol in such an unhealthy way, pretty much right from the start. I didn't know that I was turning to substances to treat my anxiety; there is so much I didn't know. And when the time is right, I will be there to talk to you and help you make right choices, and help you even more when you don't make right choices. My days are long and I am tired, but I am learning so much about being a better Mom, a better person, like the person I was when I was young, like you are.

Love you to the moon and back, Mumma

Expansion

After PDMA that morning, She walked out the back door and noticed the picture outside the art room. She had walked out that way every day at 10 am, but had not noticed the picture of the young woman with her three beautiful children. She stopped to read the plaque honoring the young woman who had tragically lost her life to addiction while her children were still so young. She saw her own little Emma in the eyes of the young twin girls and her heart overflowed and sank at the same time. The young woman standing in front of the large tree with her children was named Jennifer. She looked so vibrant and alive.

She went to the main office and asked Judy about Jennifer.

"Jennifer was an artist; it's her artwork hanging outside of the art room. Jennifer's family wanted the women at Everson to have the healing gift of art and have been longtime supporters of the program." Judy shared, "Her family lives near the ocean and Jennifer had a strong connection to this little town."

She had not yet attended an art therapy group, but now felt a connection to Jennifer and planned on going that afternoon.

She used to love drawing and painting, but had lost touch with it during her addiction. Addiction really does *take everything*. She felt intimidated walking into the art group, wondering if she had lost her creativity. Cindi, the art therapy leader, was playing soothing music and had an equally soothing presence about her.

"Art is a way to express yourself without having to use words. For me it was a road back to recovery when I felt so disconnected and hopeless," Cindi shared.

She liked Cindi's approach, that art is not about the product, but the process of freeing your mind and allowing creativity to flow. She was excited to be working with charcoal which she had not done in years. Cindi prompted her to draw an "Insides and Outsides" project, and as She began drawing, she felt an expansion, like the walls she had built up to protect herself were gently coming down. Everyone seemed to be working at their own pace. When Cindi asked if anyone wanted to share their drawing, She felt protective looking over her depiction of how she felt inside compared to how she acted on the outside; but she also felt accomplished, truly *feeling* the artwork reflected how she felt.

She stood up to share her charcoal drawing, and shared how the smudged black tears running down her face on the inside picture made her think of Jennifer. She hoped that Jennifer had found peace and was still there guiding and loving her children from the other side through her beautiful artwork. She felt some long-lost pieces of herself falling into place as she hung up her artwork in her room that night.

Instead of hanging out in the backyard after the art group, She decided to walk the Grace Trail a few times. She thought about Jennifer's family and wondered how old her kids were now. She thought about the big tree they stood in front of in the photo. *Did Jennifer have siblings? Were her parents still alive? How did they survive losing her?* Walking past the painted rocks along the trail She thought of her family and how much she and Brenda used to love coloring for hours in their blanket forts on rainy days. *How did we ever grow so far apart?* She wondered. It would be easy to take all the blame, but She remembered Diana telling someone in the group that taking responsibility for our part is different than taking blame.

"I'm taking responsibility for my mess," She whispered as she passed the "Acceptance" Rock. She thought about taking Brenda to one of those painting studios someday, just having fun and laughing like they did when they were young. She smiled thinking about taking a picture of herself with Emma and Brenda in front of a big beautiful tree.

During the evening house check, the Recovery Aid, Tina, asked about her new picture on the wall.

"That's me, inside and out, coming together, opening, expanding to let recovery in," She responded with pride. After writing in her mother's journal She wrote a thank you letter to Jennifer's family for supporting the art program and her healing.

As She came downstairs for a snack she noticed the sign on the bulletin board, *Thanksgiving Visitation Schedule.* "Wait, what? Thanksgiving!" She yelled.

In the back of her mind she knew Thanksgiving was coming up, but had pushed it back, far back. She had told herself she was not going to be here for the holiday's, but where else would she be? She turned around and went back to her room, not sure how to feel or how to be. Would She be able to see Emma on Thanksgiving? She stood looking out her third story window with a distant view of the ocean. *Jennifer loved the ocean and she was gone now; her children don't have a mother this Thanksgiving,* She thought. She crawled beneath the covers and cried. Tears for Jennifer, for Emma, for Mom, for Brenda, for herself, for people out there in the cold with no family and no hope.

Dear Emma, I Love You! I drew pictures today in an art group. Remember how much we loved drawing and fingerpainting? I can't wait to get new art supplies and work on a project together. There is so much I want to share with you and hopefully someday you will understand why I had to be away from you. I'm tired tonight, sad thinking about being here on Thanksgiving. I had told myself I would have it all figured out and be home with you by now. My counselor suggested making a gratitude list, so I'll start with one thing today. I'm grateful for my beautiful Emma! Love you to the moon and back, Mumma

Healing

Settling into her seat in the PDMA group meeting in the art class that morning, She felt like a kid again, but it was a good feeling this time. She enjoyed the smell of glue drying, paintbrushes in the sink, and art projects hanging on the wall. It brought her right back to fifth grade pottery class. *Maybe I'll be an artist*, She giggled to herself as Diana walked in. She felt a surge of hope for the future mixed with fear of actually working for something that matters so much, herself.

After the opening meditation Diana asked the group, "Which area of your recovery are you most challenged in, mind, body, or spirit?"

"I'm going to try a session with the energy healers when they come next week, maybe that will help," a woman named Pam offered.

She didn't reply but dismissed the idea of energy healers immediately for no other reason except *healing* sounded strange.

After dinner, She was alone in the backyard and heard a bird softly singing. She closed her eyes and remembered how much her father had loved listening to the birds in their backyard. He would always close his eyes and tilt his head back as if to hear them better. She tilted her head back, and warm tears rolled down her cheeks as she remembered her father. After he had passed, She had felt their father-daughter connection all around her, but then she had lost it during her addiction. She had accepted that loss as punishment for being a bad person and worked hard to keep him far from her thoughts. She had learned in group that pushing feelings away doesn't work for long and sooner or later you reach for something to numb the pain. She felt like this was one of those times. She could try and push missing her Dad away or take the leap and connect with him.

At that moment, She heard two birds singing in unison, harmonizing with each other.

She imagined that the birds were her and her dad singing and talking together as they flew overhead. She quietly whistled along with the birds, and drifted into a state of relaxation and felt what seemed like a divine presence, right there in the backyard beneath her favorite beech tree. She tilted her head back, closed her eyes, and thanked her Dad, whispering, "Talk to you soon."

She had heard the term *conscious contact* being thrown around in the literature she'd been given and again by the women on staff and in the house. She originally thought they were trying to bullshit her. She had neither understood this term, nor cared to understand. But She woke up the next morning smiling and whispered, "Good morning, Dad." All along She had been waiting for something outside of herself to *prove* a spiritual connection. Now She felt like she could actually make the connection herself anytime she wanted or needed to. Suddenly She wanted to yell from the rooftops, *This shit is real if you do the work.*

Later in the group session, new women joined them. *Here we go again,* She thought.

"I'm Katelyn alcoholic, Brittany addict, Leah alcoholic, addict."

She was starting to feel better through doing the work, but recognized that she felt annoyed by the staff's insistence on constantly using these negative labels to identify herself. It was as if reminding yourself every time you want to share something that you have trashed your life. She watched as new women were *told* this is how to self-identify. She quietly added her own encouragement and reminded them they did not have to do this, that it was time to start feeling better about themselves. She enjoyed the group and Commitment Meetings daily, but remained annoyed by what felt like a cult-like mantra of repeating the words, *I'm an alcoholic and addict. Enough already.*

During her session with Diana that week, She decided to finally confront the issue instead of grumbling about it. Diana had always told the group to speak up for themselves. She was going to take her up on the invitation.

In typical fashion, Diana replied with, "You seem annoyed by this. Why?"

"It's not about me," She replied. "Why are we basically forced to identify with negative labels which then perpetuate the already-heavy shame we carry?"

"It seems to be about you and you seem to be really angry about it," Diana calmly commented.

"It feels like punishment, like I'm bad and have this label or life sentence stuck to me. How am I supposed to feel good about myself today if I am calling myself names every time I speak in a meeting?"

"Why do you think it's a negative label? When did you first feel shame about your addiction?"

She began to cry out of sheer frustration that Diana would ask such a ridiculous question; negativity and shame were the name of the addiction game she felt.

Diana sat quietly as she always did, then asked, "Are you approaching this from an addiction or recovery perspective?"

Sitting on the yellow couch with her head as far back as it could go, She opened her eyes and noticed the last of the bright red leaves on the tree against the window. It seemed like only a few days ago the leaves were starting to turn yellow and orange, now they were so red. As the leaves gently drifted to the ground, She felt the letting go, something was letting go, shifting. She pushed the window open above her head and breathed, as if to take in the energy of the tree, gracefully letting go.

Diana led her countless layers beneath her own thought patterns to a core belief that She was no good. She had felt this way for as long as She could remember, long before her addiction kicked in.

"Do you think your three-year-old daughter Emma is no good?" Diana asked.

"Of course not!" She asserted. "Emma is perfect."

"Have you ever felt perfect?"

"Of course not." She sadly answered.

She was tired now, worn out like she had just run a race. She looked to Diana hoping they could end the session early so she could take a nap before dinner.

Sensing her exhaustion, Diana posed one last question, "Tell me one of your strengths?"

She felt at her weakest point and gave a look of *really, are you kidding?*

Diana's eyes were compassionate and her words respectfully persistent, asking in a slightly different way, "It can be something small; doesn't have to change the world. Just give me one thing about yourself you feel good about."

She heard a bird singing behind her in the tree and thought for a moment. "Pretty sure I am a kind person," She admitted.

"Put that into an 'I Am' statement," Diana suggested.

"I Am kind," She said through a grin.

"Again," Diana urged.

She said it louder and stronger each time and finally felt the truth in it.

"I am kind!" She finally giggled.

The session went fifteen minutes longer than scheduled as She came up with four more strengths she actually believed in. She thanked Diana and walked out unsure of what had just happened, but with a real smile on her face. She had demanded answers and ended up with her very own.

She sank into her seat that afternoon when she heard the 2:15 group was about family and addiction. Hadn't She talked enough about how her addiction had turned everyone in her family away in disgust? Then She heard the words *genetics* and *genogram* and something shifted. She had always thought that She was the problem in her family, but maybe there actually was more to the story. Counselor Amelia handed out a diagram to work on which detailed family members on either side of the family. She sat, unsure. It was one thing to bare her dirty secrets to people who were doing the same, but She suddenly felt protective of whatever family secrets would unfold onto the diagram in front of her. Her new roommate Amy was talking to Amelia, saying she didn't know if there was addiction in her family. Amelia told her it wasn't important to label them, but if they seemed to struggle with alcohol or drugs that was sufficient.

"Is marijuana considered a drug?" Amy asked.

"What do you think?" Amelia answered in typical fashion.

Odd how the staff consistently asked for our input when we asked a question. *Hmmmm, more ammunition for my theory of not labeling myself the dreaded alcoholic or addict,* She thought and tucked that away. She did begin to consider her father's daily drinking, and the jokes around the dinner table about his father's and his grandfathers' antics while drinking. *Maybe I'm not the only one,* She thought, as a door of curiosity began to open. *Could I have been predisposed to addiction by something other than moral leprosy and bad decisions? Imagine if all fingers were not just pointed at me, but that some of what was considered normal and even comical growing up led me onto this path.*

Her completed family tree diagram was surprisingly full of problem drinkers. As She sat back and inspected the color-coded tale of two families, she felt odd relief over the diagram. She was not the only one. She wondered if anyone else in the family had ever paid attention to the patterns that went far beyond her particular mess. Anger started to rumble around in her belly as She waited her turn to share her tragic masterpiece. By the time Amelia called on her, her anger had pretty much turned to rage.

"This is bullshit!" She shouted. "Nobody in my family ever paid attention to the problems so they just got passed down to me."

What if I could have been educated on this so-called family disease and not had to do this?

"What are you feeling?" Amelia asked.

"How do you think I'm feeling?" She snapped.

Amelia put it another way, asking, "Can you share when you have felt this way before?"

"My family never talked about anything; they yelled or ignored each other. That's it. My parents were allowed to make whatever choices and have no consequences, yet they always wanted to force punishment on me."

"How do you feel?" Amelia asked

"Lied to and abandoned," She said and wept. "Now here comes Thanksgiving and all of the family crap that comes with it."

Amelia made a suggestion. "Let's think about setting intentions this holiday season. Real intentions of how we can engage in the *spirit* of the holidays, not the usual stress. You can set an intention of being an example to your family of being truly present this year. A year they don't need to worry about you being in active addiction."

Dear Emma, as tired as I am, I love you even more! Today was a rough day, but somehow a good day all in all. I need to take a bath and go to bed soon. My mind still races trying to find a way to leave and be with you even though I know I need to be here working on getting better. I've been so used to living by impulse that it's hard to slow down and accept help. More than anything, I know that I am making changes that are going to make your life and mine so much better.

Love you to the moon and back, Mumma

Her Heart's Heart

The second Thursday of the month finally arrived, and along with it her first visit with Emma. As She came downstairs for coffee, the smell of bacon commingled with the butterflies in her stomach and she had to go outside and breathe some fresh air. The air was extra crisp and the trees were almost bare, exposing their long dark branches against the sky. She worried that Emma didn't have a warm coat that fit her. She worried that Emma wouldn't like the snack she prepared for her.

She was worried.

What if Emma was mad at her?

What if Emma had changed?

What if Emma was damaged by being with strangers?

Standing there on the front porch of the big house a mile from the beach, waiting for Emma, She suddenly couldn't breathe. Working on herself had become the norm, and day by day, she was feeling hope and confidence for a better life. *What if it's all been for nothing and Emma isn't really okay? Can life inside this bubble and the real world out there actually come together?* Fear laced with doubt moved through her like a worn, old nightmare.

"Let's go." She was startled by the booming voice of Big Sis, "Today's the day you have been working and waiting for." She was whisked down the stairs to the back yard.

The sight of Debbie pushing Jason in his stroller calmed her nerves somehow. She had volunteered to babysit an hour a week for the Moms who had their babies with them. At first, it was enough that the staff and the Moms had *allowed* her to babysit, then the Moms sought her out to spend time with their babies. Her own nurturing instinct returned when their babies smiled at her and fell asleep in her arms. Sometimes She looked at the mothers, seeing how much they loved their babies and wondered how they could sacrifice being with them by using drugs. Only to humbly realize that She had done the same. She rediscovered that she was not a terrible mother nor a terrible person.

She remembered her first Unity Group when the director said she had thought a mother's love was the strongest force on earth, but realized that active addiction is so powerful that it will even sacrifice a mother's love. When She was first separated from Emma, she had to block out the fact that it was the result of her own choices, in order to survive. Now, standing in the backyard in the shadow of the mansion, for the first time She felt humbled by the forces that had been at work in her, not humiliated.

She paced back and forth on the front porch, watching the time closely: 11 am, 11:02 am, 11:05 am. "Where is the social worker?" She grumbled. With every passing minute, it was harder to breathe. Sue the social worker pulled in at 11:10 am in a blue minivan. She ran to the car propelled by a pang of jealousy that Sue would be the one unstrapping her beautiful daughter from her car seat. Sue was pulling Emma from the car when She arrived at the minivan, overtaken with joy, fear, and unreasonable anger that Sue was handling her daughter. *Who did she think she was anyways, this is my daughter, my family!* She desperately reached for Emma, and felt her daughter squeal within their breathtaking hug.

Emma pointed at the big house excitedly, "Mummy's house, mummy's house!"

She noticed *someone* had cut Emma's hair. She also didn't recognize Emma's cute pink coat with purple flowers. Purple was Emma's favorite color. A stranger knew Emma's favorite color. A swell of anger and sadness moved through her like a tidal wave. She remembered Diana's suggestion to *just be in the moment with your baby.*

"I love your haircut, Emma," She said, breathing as deeply as she could, as if to swallow the fireball of loss she was feeling.

"Jenny took me to the big girl place," Emma giggled.

Jenny, who is Jenny? Her mind scrambled. *Jenny is the woman taking care of my daughter.*

Again, Diana's words saved her. She exhaled and leaned into Diana's words. *How wonderful it is that there are people willing to care for your child while you get better.*

"Please thank Jenny for me," She finally spoke to Sue, who smiled quietly to the side.

"Gratitude, that's what I have to hold onto," She whispered softly, twirling Emma's soft blonde curls.

"What's that?" Sue asked.

"I'm just learning so much," She said, blinking back the tears. *Smile for Emma; I love her so much*, She felt through and through and mustered her biggest smile for her daughter.

They walked inside and played for what seemed like days, but at the same time only minutes. Emma was as joyful and curious as ever which eased her guilt and shame. Her daughter was not permanently damaged by their separation. She thought back to her first day at the house, knowing that if social services had not required her to get help, She never would have had the courage to face her mistakes. She would have gone on blaming her family, social services, and whomever called to report that her daughter was unsafe. If She alone had to take responsibility amidst the searing pain of reality, She would not have survived.

"We will have to end the visit soon," Sue said, explaining that she had to get Emma back by 3:00 pm. She looked up at Sue. She hadn't noticed how young she was when they arrived. Sue had to be younger than me, all dressed up in her black blazer and pinstripe shirt, trying to look older. She wanted to get angry about this, but instead felt embarrassed that someone this young had to bring her daughter to visit her in rehab. Her mind raced wondering where Sue was taking her daughter and why it would take so long to get there. She had no idea where the foster home was and her mind began to implode with outrageous questions.

As they walked to the minivan, Emma pointed at the house again, "Stay with mummy, "beginning to squirm nervously in her arms.

"Mummy needs to stay here and get better for a little while longer," She tried to explain, mustering another smile though she felt like wailing.

Emma screamed and rolled around while Sue tried strapping her into the car seat.

She got in the minivan beside Emma and gently strapped her in, while Emma whimpered, "Mummy come home."

She held her sweet little face, looked deep into her blue eyes, "Mummy loves you so much and we will be together soon. It's ok to be sad. I miss you too."

She didn't remember much after that, Diana came out at some point and walked her back into the house, holding her by the arm which was numb like the rest of her body.

Her mind spun. *How can this be happening? How can Sue be driving off with my daughter in a blue minivan? How can strangers have my baby? How will I survive?*

Big Sis came towards her and She collapsed in her arms, convinced she would not survive the heartbreak she felt for herself and for poor innocent Emma. It was over. She was done. She gave up the fight.

The rest of the day was a blur. She slept, cried, tried to eat dinner, and was dragged to the Commitment Meeting at 7:30 pm by her Little Sis. *Imagine them making me a Big Sis to a new person,* She wondered. *Don't they know I can barely take care of myself?*

A woman named Paula showed up for the meeting with a donut shop coffee cup in hand. *How dare she bring real coffee in when we are stuck with fake crap coffee.* She wondered, relieved to feel something other than self-pity.

Paula began talking about her surrender moment, "A painful awakening to the reality of my life happened during the first month in recovery when I knew I could no longer fight against my situation, the cards I had been dealt, the past, or myself anymore."

She wanted to get up and leave the meeting but could not pull herself away from the mysterious connection she was feeling with Paula, in this room, in this house full of women. She stopped asking why, stopped wondering when, stopped trying to analyze and just sat quietly. Her sorrow had simply cracked her open to the message. As if on auto-pilot, She went up to Paula when the meeting ended and asked for her phone number. Paula wrote her number on her notebook and told her to call tomorrow when She got her phone privilege. She didn't ask guests for their numbers, but somehow she knew this woman had something that she desperately wanted and needed.

Climbing up the stairs, She saw the Recovery Bowl, filled with colorful recovery rocks with names painted on them – some sparkly, some with designs, and some plain. They all had the creative touch of the women who painted them. She had thought it was funny and took pride that She had gotten away with not painting a rock. Usually Judy was on top of all that stuff and would have been asking her *how can I help you paint your rock today*, then would have made her pick a specific time that day that she would commit to doing it. She had felt kind of special that nobody had noticed, but this morning felt sad about it. Emma had seen the sparkly rocks and had wanted to take one. She had told a white lie to Emma. *Mummy moves her colorful rock from one bowl to the other every morning to remind her that She is getting better every day and will be home soon.* She watched other women pray and move their rocks every day and now really wanted to be part of that prayer – for the strength to stay away from a drink or drug today no matter what. It was a commitment to herself and to Emma. She went back down to the art room and found the bucket filled with rocks from the beach, painted a rock purple (Emma's favorite color), and wrote her daughter's name in silver sparkles. Exhausted but grateful She fell into bed that night.

Dear Emma, today was the greatest day ever because we got to be together finally! You look so beautiful and I love your new haircut. I can tell that the nice people taking care of you really love you too. I painted a rock purple and put my name on it today. On the back of the rock I painted your name in the silver sparkles that you like so much. I will bring it home with me and we can move it every morning to remind ourselves how much we want to be together and have a good life. One of the mothers here has a card in her room that says having children is like having your heart walk around outside of your body. You are my heart, sweet Emma.

Love you to the moon and back, Mumma

The Newcomer

She had gotten into the habit of getting up early no matter how tired so that She could connect with birds in the backyard before everyone else got up. In the early morning hours, the birds seemed to be sharing secrets with their song, as if they knew there was magic in the day. She didn't want others to think she had become some strange bird lady but she felt this special, true, private connection to the birds was a connection with her Dad.

This morning, an older woman was already sitting alone in the backyard, right near her favorite beech tree. She walked down the stairs to the expansive backyard, feeling annoyed over why this woman had to be in her spot. The woman didn't even look up when She got closer and just sat with her arms folded, head down. She remembered what Judy had said about welcoming newcomers, never forgetting the pain and fear of the first day, and introduced herself. The woman still didn't look up, so She offered her a cigarette. The woman just got up and walked away slowly with a limp. She was glad to have her peaceful spot to herself. She said a quiet prayer for the new woman, then chatted with her dad through the chirping of the birds.

She didn't see the new woman at the Thought of the Day meeting or breakfast. Five minutes into the PDMA group, Judy escorted the new woman into the room, introducing her as Anna. Anna slumped into the open seat, head down, seeming annoyed and hopeless. She remembered that feeling from her first group, wanting nothing to do with anyone, anything, and not wanting to be anywhere. Diana asked Jess to read over the group rules: *Confidentiality, Equal Airtime, No Sugar Coating, etc.*

Jess went on to explain the PDMA process, "Plan, Do, Measure, Act is a check-in form used to keep us accountable for changes we commit to making towards our daily goals."

Holy shit, She thought, *THAT is what PDMA means*. Since the first group when She had decided it was stupid, through rough times when PDMA group was her life raft, during her dread over honest feedback, and finally feeling it was a safe place, She had never really thought about what the acronym actually stood for. She hoped that Anna was listening to the explanation so she could save herself two months of not knowing, or maybe not caring. After everyone else checked in, Diana asked if Anna wanted to introduce herself.

Without looking up Anna said, "You already know my name."

"Would you like to share a little about yourself? "Diana asked.

Anna sat quietly for a few minutes, the silence of the group opening a way for Anna.

"You don't want to know me," Anna said, shame and fear dripping from her words.

More uncomfortable, yet necessary silence. Then Anna let it rip, "I just got out of jail after my third arrest for drunk driving. During a blackout I crashed into a pole and almost died." Shifting back and forth in her seat, Anna continued, "I was in intensive care for a month and from there went to jail." She paused. "I'm not sure due to my blackout if I intentionally drove into the pole, trying to finally break this cycle. Can't stay sober. Can't get drunk enough to forget," her voice quivered.

The air was silent and thick with the kind of empathy that survivors share as they witness each other's pain. Anna looked up at some point, locking eyes with hers.

"I'm glad you are here, Anna," She said.

Tuesday morning, Judy handed her a packet and told her She would be sharing her story at the Heart of the House meeting next Thursday morning. For some reason, She thought she wouldn't have to tell her life story until she was getting ready to leave. *What's up with these people, write an autobiography, write your timeline, now share your story with the whole house?* She had a million questions but slowly exhaled, took the packet, and walked out of the office. Judy must have sensed her dismay and followed her out into the hallway.

"One of the miracles of the program is the honest open connections women make with each other and foundational to that is sharing your story," Judy offered.

Still numb. Numb was a reaction She often had when she stuffed her fear down. It would erupt in anger towards somebody random down the line. In the past, She would become overwhelmed and drink or use during uncomfortable situations. *Big deal*, She thought, *that's just me. I can't help it.* Later that night, She looked through the packet and felt confident that she would just refuse, or pretend to be sick that day.

Fall turned to winter now. Women spent more time indoors. She had grown used to the gossip machine; it was always running on some level, sometimes a low murmur, but during this colder indoors weather, it seemed to have grown into a deafening roar. She tuned most of it out. But when the gossip started to swirl about Anna because she was quiet and kept to herself most days, She felt protective. Horrible rumors were circulating now that Anna had killed someone in a blackout, that she was stealing cigarettes, and other cruel lies. The staff and others tried to clamp down on the rumor mill; it came up weekly now in Unity Group. *Gossip is poison, and if you have a problem with someone, you need to go to them directly.*

But a revolving door of women were afraid to actually look at themselves so they continued to point the finger at other people. *How could they not know how childish and mean they were being,* She wondered angrily. She noticed how women stopped talking when Anna walked into the room. She was sure that Anna noticed it too. Afraid of addressing it and having the rumor mill turned on her, She didn't know what to do. She reached out to Anna in her own way, but Anna clearly couldn't trust anyone.

Today in Unity Group, a lot of tension was escalating with whispers of stealing and side accusations of who was doing it. Staff had gathered with us.

Anne made a point to address the rumors, and she reminded us that stealing was an old addictive behavior and how important it was to deal with it in recovery.

Big Sis chimed in, “Whoever is stealing is actually staying in active addiction on some level. It’s safe to be honest here and really ask for help.”

Anne asked, “Give me a show of hands of anyone who had ever stolen before.”

Nearly every woman slowly raised their hands. Some slid their eyes at Anna, who sat quietly in her chair, as usual.

As everyone began to let down their hands, a woman named Shelley kept her hand up. Her voice shaking, she looked at Big Sis, “Um, so, I stole your cigarettes.”

There was a silent gasp in the room.

Shelley began to cry and slumped her head in her hands, “I just didn’t know how to ask for help and had no smokes. The last time I was in treatment I was stealing and I relapsed as soon as I left.”

Out of the silence, Big Sis put her hand on Shelley’s shoulder and offered, “I understand. Thank you for your honesty. I don’t think I have ever heard someone openly admit to stealing; that’s so brave.”

Emboldened by Shelley's honesty, two other women shared that they had shoplifted while out on pass, admitting what a rush it had been for them. She could not believe people were talking about all of this in front of staff. She realized the staff were not judging, shaming, or punishing, but trying to help the women understand how other behaviors lead back to active addiction. The mood was shifting, but Anna was still quiet in her chair.

She took a deep breath and asked, “Has anyone in the room ever been gossiped about?”

Almost every woman raised her hand.

“During my first week, I heard gossip about other women and it fueled my plan to leave. I was sure if they were talking about other people, they would talk about me and the awful things I had done,” She shared, remembering how awful it felt. “So, I planned to leave but I was lucky enough to get a miracle – hearing something that allowed me to stay one more day, then one more day. What if someone is hurting so much they miss their miracle and they leave because they are being gossiped about, and never have another chance?"

The room fell silent.

Anna slightly lifted her head in her direction. Her breath quickened with courage.

She suggested the Unity topic for the week: "Say only kind words to and about each other."

Dear Emma, thinking of you every day and getting stronger every day. I had no idea that in order to get better I have to learn to deal with feelings and situations in totally different ways than before. I am so glad I am getting help now and will be able to share these things with you. I wish you could write to me too so that someday I could understand what you went through. I know when you are older and when you read this you will understand how important it is that I am doing this now and how much it is going to make our lives better. Sleep well, sweet Angel. My bed is next to a window just like at home. I lie in bed in the mornings and watch the wind dance with the curtains just like we used to do together.

Love you to the moon and back, Mumma

Fantasy

She had blocked her ex-boyfriend on social media and had not thought of him since the *relapse* that first day with her cell phone and trying to run away with him. Two weeks later, She received a message on Facebook from a random woman's account relaying a message from Josh, Emma's Dad. She felt like she was going to throw up from the violent rush of anger, excitement, and fear. The message said he had been trying to get in touch with her and wanted to talk. She messaged back telling him not to contact her through another woman and to leave her alone. He replied with the old standby: *But it's you and me and you are special, Baby.* But when she didn't acquiesce, he quickly reverted to an uglier standby: *You are a piece of garbage and I always knew it. I'm sure the new guy you are screwing will figure it out soon too.* Horrified, She dropped her phone. It had been almost three months since anybody had spoken to her like that. For a flash of a moment, it almost felt like love. Like he must care about her if he is that angry. She soon realized she had always accepted this abusive behavior as love from men but that she no longer deserved this.

She sat in the backyard startled for a while, then pulled out her notebook and followed what one of her peers had done. She wrote Josh one final goodbye letter.

> *Dear Josh, I am sorry you are so angry at me. I know that we both had a part in this mess and, in the end, we brought out the worst in each*

other. I always felt bad that your Dad had been so abusive to you and believed that if I loved you enough I could help you heal. With everything I am learning here, I now realize that we can only heal ourselves, and this is an incredible amount of painful work. It has been hard for me to let go of the fantasy of us being a happy family with Emma, but if I don't move on, I won't get better. I hope you find happiness and healing. There is help when you are ready. Thank you for giving me the best part of yourself, our beautiful baby girl, Emma. I see you in her eyes and it warms my heart. Goodbye and take care.

She brought the letter out back, put it in the empty butt can, and lit it on fire. Watching the words burn and turn to smoke, She accepted that no words she could say to Josh would change him, and that sending it to him would only tangle her up waiting for his response. She knew she had the best part of him in their daughter. Since he was not making any effort to recover, She was actually grateful that he had made no effort with social services to see Emma. She and her daughter could move on.

During the Cognitive Behavioral Therapy group, the next day, Diana asked someone to share a challenge they had that week.

Without hesitation her hand shot up.

"My emotions bounced from jealousy, anger, fear, love, and confusion when my ex reached out to me sweetly, then quickly started verbally abusing me."

"How did you feel about yourself during this situation?" Diana asked.

"I wanted to feel strong and prove that I don't need him, but ultimately felt bad about myself and maybe I deserved it. It took time for me to realize that I no longer deserved it."

"What is the evidence that you ever deserved abuse?" Diana continued.

"All of my boyfriends have been horrible to me, and I have allowed it."

"What did you do to deserve abuse?"

"I did nothing to deserve abuse."

"When did you first remember feeling this way?" Diana gently asked.

"I always have." She was finally able to realize that not only had she *never* deserved abuse, but that she had deserved to be treated with kindness and respect. She started to feel like she was just starting to scratch the surface with this therapy stuff, feeling excited and freaked out at the same time.

She had been writing letters to Emma in her journal nightly; but for the first time, she picked up her journal and wrote for herself. Private words. Through writing, She saw her strength and growth and wanted to remember that she could make good decisions during hard times. The next morning during the PDMA group, She found herself giving feedback to newcomers and wanted to give them the hope that had been freely given to her. She wondered what other suggestions she could take that she had been resistant to. She decided to expand her horizons and attend the optional meditation group with a volunteer Buddhist monk that came on Friday afternoons. An older man walked barefoot into the living room wearing a long black robe. *He really is a monk*, She thought, as five other women settled in beside her. He had a gentle smile and suggested the six of them try and get comfortable on the meditation cushions he had brought.

"Mindfulness is being able to focus on awareness of the present moment," he said in such a way that it seemed so simple and obvious. She wondered if that's what being *present* sounded and felt like.

"We are going to practice breathing techniques that will help us reach a deep level of mindfulness. The beauty of these techniques is that you can use them anytime and anywhere in order to calm and center yourself."

As She sat and breathed, she realized she had never been still, truly still and present. She decided she liked the Buddhist monk that had taught her to breathe.

Dear Emma, I Love you! I want you to always know that when I think of you or write to you a burst of joyful love comes over me. This might sound strange, but when we were first separated it was too hard to think about you because I was so afraid and sad. I was confused about how this all happened and afraid of not being able to fix it. I didn't have any healthy ways to cope with how sad I was. Now that I am learning so much about how to handle my feelings and be healthy, I don't have to be afraid of thinking of you. Now it fills me with happiness and hope that we will be together soon and I will never mess up like this again. I learned some really cool breathing exercises to help deal with stress and I can't wait to share it with you.

Love you to the moon and back, Mumma.

Heart of the House

As Wednesday morning rolled around, She felt the old familiar numbness at the thought of having to share her personal story at Heart of the House Group. The cold November sky provided extra motivation to stay in bed warm beneath the covers. She thought of days as a child when she would try to stay home from school, just wanting to take a break from the world. She knew Judy would be even tougher to convince than her Mom, and slowly rolled out of bed. She always looked forward to morning coffee and a warm breakfast in the light-filled dining room, but not this morning. The sky was an ominous shade of gray and the strong smell of cinnamon lingering in the air from homemade French toast felt abrasive rather than comforting. The oncoming stormy weather today matched her mood too closely.

She was happy to find the backyard empty since everyone was inside enjoying breakfast. She took shelter beneath her favorite beech tree as the clouds began to drip with rain. She heard a rumble of thunder in the distance, reminding her of climbing up on the roof with her dad to watch storms come in over the ocean as a child. Her dad seemed happiest when wild weather was on the way, as if it freed his Irish spirit, or perhaps called to his restless soul. Her Mom had worked nights and never would have *allowed* her to climb the roof, nonetheless let her climb up with him. Her younger brother would wait nervously on the porch while her older sister would disapprovingly slam the door on the way in the house. Once at the top of the roof, Dad would yell, *Bring it on!*

Remembering the wild, joyful grin of her father, She raised her fist to the sky and yelled, "Bring it on!"

She was still not sure if she would share her story at Heart of the House group or try to feign sickness that day, but remembering her father had sparked something inside her.

"Are you nervous?" Jess asked after her PDMA check-in.

She just rolled her eyes, knowing that if Diana saw her she would call her out.

Sure enough Diana asked, "How did you feel the first time you attended the Heart of the House group and heard other women sharing their stories?"

She didn't answer right away. The good old' silence hung in the room as She thought about that first Heart of the House group.

"Hopeful," She finally said, looking up at Diana.

Luckily, only a fifteen-minute break lasted between the two groups so She would not have time to talk herself out of sharing her story. Three other women were also scheduled to share. Each had fifteen minutes each. She asked to go first so that she could get it over with.

She told herself, *fuck it* to feeling like her story was not good or bad enough to merit being here, took a breath, and took what felt like a leap.

She started talking about her childhood and the memories felt good. She had written it all in her autobiography, but talking about it was different.

Everything wasn't bad.

She vividly remembered being happy as a kid.

Her Dad had always told her that She was too sensitive. She remembered feeling bad and learned to push her sensitivity and her worries down. She didn't notice anyone else in her family being too sensitive and just kept trying to push her feelings further and further down. She remembered everything feeling very heavy even though nothing *traumatic* had happened, as far as she could remember. She realized she didn't remember a lot of her childhood. But She remembered that she was thirteen when she'd had her first drink and that it had surely felt like no big deal to her. That first drink was remembered vividly. Her Dad drank every night and didn't seem to have a problem. It's just what was done in her family.

"The feeling of that first drink, it was like something magical had happened and all of my heaviness lifted. Totally gone. I don't remember everything that happened that night but I ended up throwing up and passing out. But the best part of that night was that I didn't FEEL anything. I wasn't too *sensitive anymore*, not worried, angry, afraid, or anything."

As She heard herself speaking the words aloud, she understood, for the first time, how it had all begun and why.

"I was free. Drinking was the answer. I was sure of it!" She paused. The rain pattered outside, drumming on the French patio doors behind her. Then she continued, "Knowing there was an escape through alcohol in my annoying world of adolescent insecurity, confusion, and anxiety changed my life. I drank any chance I got and truly didn't understand why anyone would *not* drink."

She remembered overhearing her mother talking about her best friend's boyfriend who was an alcoholic and what a problem he was. She vividly remembered how sure she was that the day would never come when she didn't drink, no matter what, because it allowed her to be comfortably in her own skin, for once.

"That was the beginning of losing my freedom," She admitted.

The women in the group were listening intently and nodding their heads as if they truly understood. She felt supported, heard, and seen. It was a strange, wonderful feeling, and not scary. All along, her biggest fear had been the anxiety of being seen, really seen. If you don't have any idea of who you are and what you think you know is ugly, how do you survive other people seeing you? She continued to share her story about how her transition to using drugs because friends had called her a lush and told her she was sloppy when she drank had felt like a reasonable choice. Through abusive relationships, attempts at treatment, managing to white-knuckle it through the unexpected pregnancy, losing custody of Emma, and an overdose, She made it through her story with two minutes to spare.

Then unexpectedly, She said, "Dad."

The room held her in their silence.

"My dad died two years ago." She exhaled. "I was with him when he took his last breath. He had been sick for so long, the coroner said it was *alcohol-related* even though his liver was fine. The doctor said the alcohol affected his brain and other parts of his body." She had never talked about this to anyone, not even Diana.

"I was there with him in the end from 7:00 am when the hospice nurse called us, until 9:00 pm when he finally passed. I felt him *pass* – he was there in his withered broken body one moment, then his breath and spirit were gone from his body and his spirit filled the room. I sensed him rise up to a higher plane and knew from that moment on we would have a better relationship. He would not be wounded, angry, unpredictably wonderful and funny one minute then raging and blaming the next. He had a sweet and kind soul that did not receive the nurturing love for his unique spirit due to his parents' wounds and addictions. He was a wounded child to the end, one that I was not able to save no matter how I tried. I didn't know how to process the grief, and instead followed down the road of addiction after him. I lost my connection to my dad during my active addiction and have been punishing myself up until now. From outside on this stormy day She heard a bird calling to her and smiled knowingly.

"My Dad's burdens got the best of him and I am determined not to let that happen to me. I thought it was all over when I turned 30, but I realize I have time to turn things around." She looked up as if in a trance; the women were in silent reverence, some crying, some nodding. She had never spoken of her dad before, burying herself and her grief as deeply as she could.

"Thank you for listening," She gracefully concluded.

She had been putting off calling Mom about Thanksgiving, not wanting to feel badly for being in treatment during the holidays. She talked in the PDMA group about feeling angry – that it's just not supposed to be the way you spend a holiday, in treatment. A message from Mom was delivered to her and as she stared at the paper, it forced her to finally face reality. Mom wanted to let her know that she had left a message for the social worker, asking if she could bring Emma for a visit on Thanksgiving, but hadn't heard back. *Thanksgiving is tomorrow. That's bullshit.* She thought, crumpling the message and throwing it in the bushes. She had been avoiding the whole holiday thing and hadn't tried to arrange the visit herself. She wanted to scream, scream at her Mom, scream at the social worker, scream at someone!

She hated how good she could feel at one minute, then shitty and terrible the next.

She needed to feel different and was afraid of making an impulse stupid decision.

"What am I supposed to do?" She mumbled, "I can't handle this; but no one to blame but myself."

She stood at the large stained glass window on the second floor landing, looking out at the street. *What's out there?* She thought, *If I leave ... just walk down the street ... I will be free, and I'll just figure it out.* The road was slightly blurry through the colored glass. She couldn't see clearly inside or out. She followed the impulse, *just go*.

She walked down the carpeted winding stairs, out the front door, down the four large granite steps, and across the lawn. She got to the entrance of the Grace Trail and stopped cold in her tracks. *Just go*, She thought, *maybe I am supposed to walk this off, as Judy says, not walk off!* She looked back at the towering mansion against the cold November sky, clouds drifting gently above. The lonesome sound of a distant dove called her to turn and walk to the left. She pulled her hoodie up over her head and walked into the wind, and then followed the Grace Trail, as it wound in a big circle around the house and annex, the marshland out back, past the dumpster, along the main street, by the staff parking lot, and finally, by the "Believe" rock. She lost count of how many times she circled it. Her lungs stretched with Autumn's brisk air, reminding her with each breath, *I am alive.* By dusk, She had walked off the confusion, anger, pain, and sadness.

"Happy Thanksgiving," Judy said with a smile, as she waved to her from the parking lot, walking to her car. "See you tomorrow."

"You're working tomorrow?" She asked, surprised.

"Of course," Judy answered, turning back to meet her on the path, "I'll put my turkey in the oven in the morning, then come in for the clothing auction, which will be fun. We collect the nicer donations all year and everyone gets something nice for the holidays."

“Why would you spend your holiday here?” She asked, still confused.

“Everson is one of my favorite places to be on a holiday.” Judy walked closer to her, tugging her coat around her shoulders. “There is a peaceful, loving, energy here that comes from the unconditional connection we all have with each other. Without all of the family drama and stress of the holiday’s we all get to focus on what really matters.”

She shrugged, “I guess that's true.”

Judy noticed her reticence. “Not being with your family on Thanksgiving can be challenging for sure. But just look at it as an opportunity to gather with your Everson family and intentionally focus on your blessings, not your problems.” Judy waited as the words sank in. “Plus, you’ll get extra phone time and you get to sleep in!” Judy winked.

“That’s for sure!” She replied with a laugh, imagining a rare lazy morning. Then she put a hand on Judy's coat arm. “I am grateful for you,” She said, realizing this would be her first Thanksgiving sober.

Dear Emma, I wish so much that I could hug you and read you a bedtime story tonight. I got so sad today that we couldn't be together on Thanksgiving that I wanted to leave. I know if I leave now, we can’t be together. I need to be strong and not give up. It’s weird how doing the really hard things ends up making you feel better. That’s probably what being strong means.

I did talk about my Dad today. It was hard and sad, but it felt so good to finally be able to talk about him. I miss him so much; he always made me laugh and we had the same sense of humor. You were only a baby when he died; he loved you so very much. He used to lay on the ground with you and just stare into your eyes with the biggest smile. I am beginning to feel his spirit with me again and it feels wonderful. I am also beginning to forgive myself for making such a mess of our lives.

Love you to the moon and back, Mumma

Fullness

Thanksgiving came and went with new traditions and lessons on gratitude. Even though it seemed so obvious, She had never connected the link between Thanksgiving and gratitude. Three women from the community came in for a special morning Gratitude Meeting. They handed out little cards with two short sentences and everyone read them out loud: *Gratitude unlocks the fullness of life. It turns what we have into enough.*

"Close your eyes, and feel these words filling you up as I read them quietly," the older woman Charlotte suggested, "Gratitude unlocks the fullness of life, it turns what we have into enough."

She silently wept as a calm sense of grief and release moved through her. She had been anticipating feeling horrible today on *a family holiday.* In this moment, She felt like she was right where she was supposed to be.

"Thank you," She whispered, looking up to catch Charlotte's warm smile. She wondered why they didn't identify as alcoholics and addicts like everyone else that comes in for meetings.

"Good morning, and thank you for sharing your Thanksgiving with us," Charlotte shared. "We are from a local Al Anon support group for families of people with addiction. Addiction is a family disease and everyone is affected in some way. Our mission is to help families and friends of alcoholics/addicts find hope and encouragement to live joyful serene lives."

"Can anyone attend an Al Anon meeting?" Sarah asked, "Even alcoholics?"

"Yes," Charlotte answered, "anyone that has been affected by someone else's addiction can benefit from the shared experience and support of others who are learning to set boundaries and develop healthy coping skills. We have sponsors, work with the same twelve steps, and have anonymous support group meetings."

"This feels like a missing piece," She mumbled before realizing she had spoken aloud.

"Did you want to share?" Charlotte asked.

She leaned forward in her chair, "The genogram assignment we did last week … I've kind of known there was a lot of drinking in my family, but never realized how much of an impact that has had on my life, my choices, and my taking on all of the blame in my family."

"Family disease, family recovery," Charlotte nodded. "The good news is that – through Al Anon – I have learned whether or not the alcoholic in my family recovers, I can recover. I set healthy boundaries and use the tools I have learned to work on myself and recover my own wellbeing and peace."

These three women had a peace about them that *was* special. Forty women of all ages, backgrounds, and traumas crammed into the dining room where art projects and a Twelve Step poster adorned the walls. Thanksgiving was peaceful this year, and that was special too.

Everyone got sparkly warm sweaters or slippers from the auction; the traditional turkey dinner and pumpkin pie were especially delicious; family FaceTime calls were made leaving many grateful for missing the family drama; and the women shared their gratitude for each other and how it helped them stay sober another day. She thought back to what Anne said in the Unity Group about *the opposite of addiction is connection.* She reflected on how isolated and alone she had felt in the shame of her active addiction, like nobody would ever understand. Looking around the dining room now, while everyone ate leftover pie, She felt connected – truly connected – more than she ever had to her own family. She thought about family members that she hadn't seen in a long time due to her addiction, and began to feel a nervous excitement to reconnect.

Friday afternoon, She was sent to Diana's office and it felt good not to wonder if she had done anything wrong. Diana's unusually serious look worried her as She walked into the small office.

"Your Mom is on the phone, "Diana said, pushing the speaker button.

Mom's voice was quivering, "Grampy has died, he had a massive stroke last night, went into a coma, and just passed."

Her body became numb and She began to rock back and forth, not able to process what She was hearing. She saw Diana reach out and put her hand on her arm, but she could not feel anything. She had not seen Grampy in over a year because she could not bear the disappointment he must have had towards his favorite granddaughter. He was the only one that seemed to truly understand her: they laughed at the same corny jokes and always had fun together. After Emma was born and She had started drinking, her priorities slowly slipped away as did her connection to her beloved Grampy.

"Why didn't you let me know about the stroke last night?" She yelled at her Mom, feeling as if this was some sort of punishment.

"They thought he was going to stabilize and I didn't want to upset you unnecessarily."

"It was necessary," She cried, "I am necessary!" She slammed the receiver down.

A group of women had gathered outside the door and tried to console her as She burst out of the office.

She retreated to the big closet in Room 23, sinking into the corner where nobody could find her. Her insides felt like a bomb had gone off and She could not collect the pieces. When her father had died from *alcohol related causes,* Grampy had been her only comfort and safety. He always saw and accepted her for who She was. Grampy was the one that helped her reconnect to her Dad though the birds he loved so much. She had been working on a project in art therapy to give to Grampy when she got out. Everything was spinning amidst the torturous combination of raw and numb. *Numb*, a voice piped into her mind, *I could help you get numb enough if you want.* She spun her head around as if to find someone there, in the seductive voice of her old abusive friend, Addiction.

Big Sis found her. She gently knocked and then walked in the closet, sat beside her, and said nothing. She sat rocking back and forth trying to decipher the offer in her head to numb out completely. Big Sis was leaving soon to go to another sober house but had heard about Grampy's passing, so she searched for her. Knowing that no comforting words could ease the shocking pain, they just sat together, breathing.

"You have grown so much, Little Sis, since the day you walked in, not wanting anything to do with anything," Big Sis offered as some sort of comfort. "I knew right where to find you because this is where you would hide out those first days when you didn't know what else to do. You have truly been a reminder and an inspiration of how much courage it takes to walk in and do the hard work of change, recovery."

She didn't dare look up because she had no words, just swirling old familiar thoughts of using and leaving.

"Remember," Big Sis reminded, "we are granted the miracle of willingness during the lowest point in our lives and together, united we recover, a day or a moment at a time."

She sat in silence, secretly hoping Big Sis would know how badly she wanted to use and numb out right now. Her eyes looked pleadingly at her. Big Sis registered it with a knowing nod.

"How could the wretched thing that took your daughter away and brought you here disguise itself as a solution to you now, as a friend in a time of need? Just for today, we don't pick up a drink or a drug, no matter what!" Big Sis held her in a big long hug. After a few minutes, she said, "Come find me if you can't sleep, and remember, you will get through this and you are not alone."

As much as She wanted to be alone, left alone, she knew the women of this house had her back without any ulterior motives. She debated going downstairs, yet felt stuck within her own pain. A familiar feeling. She thought about the gratitude quote and then, *The fullness of life feels really heavy right now.*

"You'll feel the fullness of joy and sorrow in recovery," She mumbled, now mocking Charlotte's words. "Fuck that."

She had never actually tried praying for something, but slowly moved to her knees and prayed to her Grampy, asking for the courage to move forward, knowing it was what he would want for her. She soon felt a sense of comfort come over her. She went downstairs to the Commitment Meeting. The woman, Kate, whose number she had gotten that first night in the meeting – but had never called – was there. Warmly, she found her and told her how wonderful it was that She was still there.

Without even thinking, She blurted out "Will you be my sponsor?"

Kate replied just as quickly saying, "Of course. But know that you have to call me daily to check in."

Kate gave her homework to start reading the Big Book. "It's where all recovery begins, at the beginning."

That sounded like something Grampy would say, and in that moment, She knew her prayer to her Grampy had been answered. Now She had a sponsor.

When She was changing for bed she found the note from Diana that Big Sis had given her earlier that day. *It's time to set up a family meeting. Friday works best for me; let's schedule it tomorrow.* A family visit sounded like a nice thing, for other people. The thought of it caused her anxiety though. She already knew that she'd fallen behind over the holiday. Three times this week, Judy had spoken to her about why She was not making her bed and that her chore hadn't been done on time. She knew she was pulling back, that she dreaded the next step coming.

When Diana first suggested a family meeting with her mother and sister, she assured her everyone would have an equal chance to talk; but it felt like everything over the years had already been said. She felt embarrassed for hanging up on her Mom earlier, not considering how her Mom and Brenda were handling Grampy's death. Brenda was closer to him than anyone, but at least she had gotten to be with him. *Nobody even let me know it was happening till after he was gone.* Amidst the swirling feelings of guilt, sadness, anger, grief, and regret, She realized she could not blame anyone else for her missing out on important things. Staff here talked about the self-centeredness of people in addiction and early recovery. She had shrugged it off as not pertaining to her, but now she was starting to see that it did. She slowly opened to the idea of a family meeting.

Dear Emma, today was a really hard day. My Grampy, your great Grandfather died and I almost couldn't handle it. I wasn't able to be there for your Nana or Auntie and just retreated out of guilt for not being there for him, with him. Instead of apologizing, I got mad. It's hard learning how to handle feelings, but I am getting better at it. I even got a sponsor today, someone to talk to who will help me make the right choices. I miss you. This is so intense, but we will never have to be apart again. Love you to the moon and back, Mumma

Light

She woke up feeling restless and annoyed. It seemed as if every day was getting colder, the trees were stark, and the pretty colored leaves were crumpled and gone. The coffee had been weak of late. She was quiet during the PDMA group and didn't feel like *dealing* today.

A woman named Julie shared, "A bed at a sober house opened earlier than expected and I'll be leaving tomorrow."

She felt a pang of jealousy that Julie was getting to leave early and not her.

"Congrats," She said to Julie, who quickly picked up on her flat tone.

"What's going on? "Julie asked, "You've been so quiet; are you annoyed?"

With only a couple of minutes left in the group, She brushed it off, not wanting to get feedback today, "Just tired."

She walked outside right after the group, zipping her sweatshirt up to her neck. Julie followed behind her, handing her a warmer house coat from the front foyer.

"Are you feeling stuck?" Julie asked. "You should take the energy healing session I signed up for before knowing I was leaving early. You want it?" Without thinking, She agreed to the session, just wanting Julie to leave her alone. She had resigned herself to the misery of this upcoming family meeting, and was in fuck-it mode.

She had no idea what energy healing was, but had enjoyed breathing and weekly meditations with the Buddhist monk. *So how bad could this be?* She also knew at least a dozen other women wanted to have a healing session but there wasn't enough room. Maybe Grampy was opening the door for her again. She felt a twinge of excitement about tomorrow's new experience and leaned into it. Big Sis had talked about gratitude being a feeling of thankfulness at times, and other times it was a choice.

Later, she climbed into the car with an RA named Shirley. She had to admit that she was relieved to be getting out of the house for a while, even if it was to go to the dreaded dentist. She had been really good at making sure Emma went to the dentist, but had ignored her own dental problems. *Who likes the dentist?* She thought, shrugging off the guilt of yet another thing she had not dealt with.

"Pain sure is a great motivator," Shirley commented, "Buckle up, let's go."

"Is there any other motivator?" She laughed.

"Yes," Shirley answered, "that's what PDMA group is for, setting goals every day, large or small, and taking action based on choice not crisis."

"You should put that on a bumper sticker, Choice not Crisis," She replied.

Two hours later - with one tooth filling and one drooling numb face – She walked up the four large granite steps into a Christmas explosion.

"What happened? She yelled, overwhelmed by the nine-foot Christmas tree, giant red bows, and jingle bells ringing through the air. Flashes of little Emma lying beneath the Christmas tree looking up at the colorful lights felt like shock waves.

"I'm not ready for this, we just got through Thanksgiving," She yelled at Judy in the main office.

Judy looked up from tying gold bows.

"What's happening?" She demanded.

"I'm tying bows for the staircase," Judy replied.

"No, I mean, why now?"

"We decorate for Christmas the week after Thanksgiving. It is a nice tradition. Enjoy it; this is your home while you are here."

Her alarm bells of fear and guilt urged her to run, to leave the constant reminder of another holiday here and not in her own home with Emma. As she headed to the front door, the words of "O Holy Night" surrounded her: *Fall to your knees, Oh hear the angel voices.* She wandered back to Judy's office, sliding into the chair beside the desk.

"That's my favorite Christmas song. I played it for Emma as a lullaby every night before bed, even when it wasn't Christmas. How am I supposed to handle this? I can't be away from her." She implored.

"O Holy Night is one of my favorite songs too," Judy said calmly. "Think of the lyric, *Till he appeared and the soul felt its worth.* You are showing up, facing difficult realities, healing, and feeling your worth. Life's challenges do bring us to our knees. Spirituality meets us there, on our knees, and gives us the grace to rise up, stronger than ever."

"But the tree – Emma's favorite thing is lying under the tree and looking at the lights," She whimpered.

"Yes, and when she visits next week, you can both lie under the tree and look at the lights, and talk about new Christmas traditions, hopes, and dreams for the future. You are getting through this and you don't have to do it alone, ever," Judy assured.

Big Sis rushed into the office, looking for her. "Nice face, how much Novocain did they give you?" They laughed as She grimaced. Big Sis pulled her up by the arms. "C'mon, you survived the dentist; now let's go find Santa!"

Arm in arm with Big Sis, She headed out to the Everson Christmas Village, never so grateful for Big Sis's pushy insistence as she was that day.

"Everyone in the Energy Healing Group needs to meet in the living room at 10:15," Judy announced during breakfast Tuesday morning.

She headed to the living room for her session, and there the smell of incense was thick in the air. She took a deep breath, inhaling the earthy scented air, evoking a deep sense of nostalgia, for what She was not sure of.

"Welcome, do you hug?" A woman in a maroon sweater dress, black tights, and no shoes cheerily welcomed her in. She had never been hugged so tightly.

After hugging all twelve women, including Diana, she said, "Welcome, I am Ariel, and this is my brother Jacob. We are healers. I've done energy healing work with a young woman who went through Everson last year. She's found her freedom from old addictive patterns through energy work. Energy can become blocked due to trauma and addiction. We work to clear and balance that energy and bring in more light and joy."

Luckily someone in the group shot their hand up asking, "What do you mean by light?"

"Good question," Ariel answered, "Light is simply positive energy. We believe light is spiritual energy that propels the life force of goodness and love to all creation, a conduit of consciousness. Light is one of the most universal and fundamental symbols of goodness. It is the spiritual and the divine; it is illumination and intelligence. Light is the source of goodness and the ultimate reality."

Jacob added, "We are going to awaken your divine blueprint and heighten your connection with your highest self, bringing in and anchoring more light. This gives you the ability to make decisions based on your individual life's purpose."

How odd, She thought, listening with an ear of suspicion but also veiled hope. Purpose sounded like a word from a foreign language. She had always drifted from thing to thing, person to person, problem to problem with no purpose or direction. *Isn't that what life is*, She wondered, *survival and having fun when you can?*

Ariel then explained that they would be receiving a Life Activation session which would reconnect them to their original soul blueprint. "Kind of like a spiritual factory reset," she said with a chuckle.

As strange as the ideas seemed, She felt deep inside that her original *blueprint* – whatever that was – surely could not have been to crush her life under the weight of addiction.

"Bring it on," She exhaled and got up.

Eyes closed, She stood in place and felt like *something* was moving. *Shifting* was the word Jacob used. She wasn't sure what was shifting, but she felt calm, like something had lifted and an open space remained in its place. Ariel moved behind her during the seated part of the session and it felt as if something *light* was moving into the newly-opened space. She felt a feeling that might have been best described as peace, for the first time. She was being bathed in a warm loving light. As She left the session room, Anna was walking in and asked her how it was. She had no words, and just told her that it was a feeling She had never felt before.

Judy called her into the office to give her a message, "You look so different, so light."

She took the folded message and walked to the back yard. Sitting under her beech tree, She looked up at the cloudy sky wondering if there had always been so many amazing shades of white, blue, and gray clouds. She could smell the salty ocean air and it felt sparkly in her lungs. She stared down at her hands. There was a beauty surrounding her that felt also somehow part of her, inside her. She opened the message from Diana: *The family meeting has been moved up to this afternoon due to your mother's work schedule.* She was surprised at the sense of happiness to see her Mom and sister. She got up and headed to the porch to wait for them.

In the rocking chair on the front porch, She watched the world go by, waiting for Mom and Brenda. She wondered if the people driving by – rushing to work or headed for a walk on the beach had any idea what was going on in this house. She had the thought that the same birds that sang from the trees in other people's backyards also sang here for her, encouraging her to keep fighting for her life. These walls witnessed so much trauma and heartache, along with countless daily miracles. Miracle after miracle of courageous women, against all odds, rising back up, finding their spark of life, and recovering their lives and their families.

"I am at the right place, at the right time," She whispered, rocking back and forth.

Just then, Mom's white Subaru pulled in. She took a deep breath and trusted this was the right time to reconnect with her family. She didn't remember her mother looking so old, so worn, as she walked up the pathway, wringing her hands. Her sister Brenda walked a few steps behind, frantically texting someone, then tucking her phone in her back pocket. Brenda looked thin and frail, her brown hair pulled into a tight ponytail to match her tight frown. She walked down the four stone steps to meet them.

Her heart rose up in her chest as she reached out to hug her Mom, suddenly terrified that she may not return the hug.

"I've missed you," her mother returned her hug and whispered while squeezing her extra tight.

She stepped back, hoping to hug Brenda, who was back on her cell phone, looking aggravated.

"Brenda put the phone away," Mom said with irritation.

It felt kind of good to hear Mom irritated at someone else besides her.

Then Diana stepped out, motioning them to come into her office, "Welcome to Everson! Hope the drive wasn't too bad; bridge traffic can be tough."

She was glad Mom took a seat on the yellow couch below the window, her favorite spot in Diana's office. It always helped her when She was feeling anxious. Brenda hurried in the door and sat in the black wooden chair beside the couch. She was surprised Brenda didn't sit next to Mom on the yellow couch. She noticed the tension between them and wondered if it had always been there. That left her the black wooden chair next to Diana. She had never sat in that chair and was surprised how comfortable it was. She was prepared for an awkward silence and had become used to it in the PDMA group. Diana jumped right in asking her to share about her experience at Everson. She had put thoughts in writing a few days ago in preparation for this meeting. Then She was riddled with nerves, and anger, but had forgotten all about it.

"Thank you for driving all the way to the Cape. I have missed you," She expressed.

She noticed a tear in her mother's eye and a scowl on her sister's face. Looking down at her hands – like She had in the backyard earlier – She felt grounded and safe within herself.

"I am here," She whispered to herself.

"Oh, there she goes; it's always about you!" her sister mumbled in return.

"Brenda!" Mom yelled, "I told you to just listen."

"No, Mom, it's okay." She spoke up. "I am ready to hear what you and Brenda have to say to me. I know I've messed up. I can't deny that anymore. I am really working on changing this time. I realize I have never stopped long enough to learn how to handle my emotions without self-destructing. When I went to treatment before, I just went through the motions with no plan to stop or change. It's not just about being sober; the work here is about learning to identify and change unhealthy patterns. Some of them I have had my whole life."

"So you are blaming me?" Mom said, choking tears back.

"No, of course not, nobody forced me to make the choices I did. For once I am taking responsibility and doing the work." She replied.

"Would you each be willing to share your hopes and concerns?" Diana prompted.

The room was silent. Diana's office had never felt so small and cramped, like the walls were closing in. She imagined the Buddhist monk sitting on the floor on his meditation pillow, showing her how to breathe and be present within.

"Breathe," She whispered.

"What's that?" Brenda yelled. "Why do you keep mumbling? If you have something to say, just say it; we drove all the friggin' way here!"

"I understand why you're upset, Brenda," She offered, "and I appreciate you traveling to see me. I am working on handling anxiety and anger through meditation and grounding techniques; that is what I am doing."

"You're angry?" Brenda laughed, "What about us and all that you have put us through over the past ten years?"

"Stop it, Brenda," Mom pleaded.

"That's right, just keep sweeping it under the rug and pretending everything is okay," Brenda said with disgust.

"We are all raw and emotional with Grampy's passing," Mom insisted, looking at Diana pleadingly. "Can we just listen to the counselor and answer her questions?"

She looked over at her sister Brenda, who looked more scared now, than angry, her lower lip quivering. She felt a wave of compassion for her sister. Her sister was right; it had been *all about her* for a long time, and it was time to own that and listen to them.

Diana nodded to Mom who nodded back in relief. Then Mom shared,

"You have no idea what it has been like wondering when the phone rings if it was going to be the call that your daughter has overdosed and died. Imagine if it were Emma, and you were helpless to stop her from self-destructing. And how would I explain to Emma if you chose that life over her?"

She felt the urge to run, disappear, defend herself, and cry.

Instead, She closed her eyes for a moment and then responded, "I can't even begin to imagine the horror of that, I *am* sorry. I know apologies don't mean anything after all of these years. I've learned that real change and time are the only amends I can make. I want a better life and realize that I have to basically change *everything* to make that happen."

"What's different this time?" Brenda asked with less venom in her voice.

"I am doing the work, really opening up and changing the way I think and act. It sucks a lot of the time and sometimes I don't want to do it; but I also feel better, stronger, and have hope for the first time that things will get better. Things are getting better. And I will do anything for Emma. She deserves a healthy mother and I know that I can't control what her Dad does."

"You sound different," Brenda said. "You aren't yelling and blaming everyone else."

"What do you want from … or for your sister?" Diana asked.

Brenda looked confused, "It's been so long since I could depend on my sister. I don't know how to answer that. I guess I miss her and I can't deal with wondering if she is going to ever get better."

Diana looked at Brenda in her compassionate way as they all sat together, in the silence.

"I miss my sister. I want her back. I want her back." Brenda admitted.

Mom reached for a tissue and dabbed at her eyes as if to stop the tears from coming.

"It seems like we are all on the same page," Diana observed. "Recovery is a way of life and a *showing*, not telling that things are going to be different. She is doing the work of building a strong recovery foundation and gaining tools to support lasting change."

She nodded in agreement, knowing it would take time for her family to see the changes and someday trust her. She was not in a rush today to try and make them understand what She was going through. Their honesty felt supportive because She had finally learned to be honest with herself.

"This is the first time being in the room with you that you're able to sit quietly and listen," Mom commented, her expression softening, her hands now relaxed in her lap.

She had become used to slightly awkward silences and realized her family had not.

Brenda jumped in to fill the silence asking, "How much longer will you be in treatment?"

"However long it takes," She replied, much to her own surprise. "Recovery is not a thing you do, but a way of life and that it takes practice and ongoing support."

She heard the words coming out of her mouth and turned to Diana who looked at her like a proud mother, something She had not seen in a very long time.

Soon, the conversation switched to Emma and how amazing she is.

"Emma loves to paint and draw just like you did as a child," Mom said proudly, "I'm adding Emma's artwork to the collection of your artwork I've saved since pre-school."

Her heart melted, having no idea Mom had saved her artwork. This must be the light that Ariel was talking about. She hadn't thought about how much She loved painting and drawing in years.

Dear Emma, I Love You! I am so tired, but so calm and happy. There is so much going on, sometimes I can't keep up. We decorated the house for Christmas today. I was really sad at first because I wanted to be decorating with you. I can't wait for you to visit; we have four Christmas trees, inside and outside! I told my social worker how much you love "O Holy Night" so your foster person can play it for you. I saw Nana and Auntie Brenda today; they miss you and love you too! It seems like we all need healing and I am glad that they visited. I had an energy healing session today; not sure exactly what happened, but I feel lighter, hopeful, and myself again. I have made a lot of real friends here and we laugh and just be silly a lot; it feels really good. Can't wait to hug you soon.

Love you to the moon and back, Mumma

A New Story

She was helping a new woman Tara with her Building History timeline when Judy called her into the office, saying she needed help with something.

"Because you have become a leader in the house you will be moving to a single room on the third floor."

She had become so used to sharing a room that the thought of having her own space thrilled her and made her a little nervous at the same time. She hoped the new room would have a distant ocean view.

When She exited the office, Tara called her back over, asking for help with her timeline because there were things she was sure she could not share.

"The more honesty you put into the timeline, the more you'll learn about your addictive patterns. You don't have to go into detail about traumatic events." She assured Tara.

Given Tara's worried look, She added, "You can tell me first … if that would help?"

Tara was frail and timid-looking, her ears poking through thin, brown shoulder -length hair.

"I struggled with an eating disorder prior to my drinking problem, and since detox I have been obsessing again about food and calories," Tara said with her head down.

"You can talk to your counselor, for sure. I've also heard other women sharing similar struggles as well. I'll attend the Body Image Group with you … if that would make you more comfortable?"

"Will I ever be comfortable?" Tara asked, "I never have been".

Friday morning, She encouraged Tara to attend the Body Image Group in the dining room. She was surprised to see the director, Anne, walk in to run the group.

Anne shared that she had been a counselor at the program years ago and loved running this group when her schedule allowed it. They read from a one-page handout simply titled, "Body Image." Body image is described as how you feel in your body when you move, a person's perception of their physical self, the thoughts and feelings – positive, negative or both – and the way we talk to ourselves in relation to our bodies.

"I don't remember a time when I didn't feel uncomfortable in my body. When I started drinking, I finally found relief," Sonya shared. "Sober though, I'm uncomfortable all over again.

Jill agreed and commented, "When things feel out of control, the only thing that makes me feel better is to restrict food. I can't do that now, so everything seems out of control."

Tara raised her hand and timidly shared, "Every time I try to get sober my eating disorder returns. It's like it just keeps switching on, keeping me sick."

"Recovery is about approaching wellness on all levels, not separately dealing with one behavior then another, but opening up to healing as a whole," Anne compassionately explained.

"But how?" Tara questioned.

"Close your eyes and relax, sink into your body sitting in the chair right here, right now," Anne instructed. "This is your one body, strong and unique, to get you through this life. Imagine accepting your body in this moment, perfect as is. Picture yourself as a little girl: would you be mean to her because of her body shape? When you are walking, resting, breathing, thank your body for being there for you every moment along the way. As you apply yourself to the work you are doing at Everson, include thanks and forgiveness to your body. You are a miracle."

She could hear Tara quietly weeping and put her hand on hers.

"You are not alone," She assured her.

"Thank you," Tara whispered.

That night in her very own tiny single room, She lay on the bed under the open window feeling the cold breeze drifting in. *Has the air always smelled this good or had something changed?* She remembered a time not too long ago when all she knew was being uncomfortable, whether high or sober. *Sober*, the word lingered in her mind. She had never been sober. She had only tried to stop for everyone else, not believing it was possible to ever be *comfortable.* She hated the word *clean* too – people referring to their clean time, like they had been dirty in active addiction. The program director talked about active recovery in Unity Group every week. The director explained, *you are either in active addiction, or active recovery, there is not a space between.* This had annoyed her for the longest time because She had lived in that space between, not able to find her place on either side.

She thought of the story Judy had told her about the young woman who overdosed three days before graduating. She imagined the young woman sitting at a desk excited to be moving on, not knowing that one relapse would be the end for her. She prayed – for her, for her family, for Judy, for Emma, and for herself. From her tiny single room on the third floor of this mansion up in the treetops, She gave herself an ounce of credit for finally taking action. Yes, She had gotten herself into this, and was now doing the work every day to get out.

She rolled over and pulled out the smooth leather tree-of-life journal. It had been a long and strange day. She wanted to really remember it. *Maybe this is what joy i*s, She thought. She wrote energy healing on her gratitude list, and then wrote out *feeling good within myself even though life is still life*. She loved the idea that energy healing opened the door to herself, reconnecting to passions and motivations to change and grow.

As She was putting her notebooks in her cute little desk, She smiled as she found the timeline she had made to help her with her autobiography. When she was having a hard time writing her life story, Big Sis had told her that it helped her to write a timeline of things not to forget. Looking at the scratched attempts in the notebook, She realized the past had been brought up to date with her autobiography. Maybe She could now write a new story, pulling out a fresh notebook, writing at the top: Chapter 1, I Am Here.

Dear Emma, exciting news, I got my own room today. It is a pretty little room on the third floor, high up in the treetops. It's cozy, and mine for now. I wish I could see your room. When we are back together, we will paint your room purple, your favorite color. I am excited to read to you before bed and tuck you in. Remember how you always insisted on reading three stories before you would go to sleep? Maybe we can read five when I get home. I started writing a story tonight about my journey back to you, back to myself, here at Everson. It feels like I am getting back to things I love and reconnecting to who I am.

Love you to the moon and back, Mumma

Envy

She was excited to wake up in her new room and looking forward to Wednesday's breakfast of homemade muffins. She giggled at the simple pleasures in her life today.

Downstairs, She saw Trisha sitting on the living room couch with her head in her hands and sat next to her.

"You don't want to miss the homemade blueberry muffins; let's go," She chirped.

"I can't eat. I'm freaking out about my family meeting with my boyfriend, Dave, and Diana this afternoon," Trisha mumbled through cupped hands.

She felt a twang of aggravation that Trish's boyfriend was allowed to visit since the visitation rule is family only.

"I was almost hoping Diana would say no to his request; but since we were living together with our son Chase, they considered him family. Dave is in treatment at the men's program and thinks he's Mister Sobriety. I know he is going to insist on being honest about what happened, and I haven't been."

"Do you trust Diana?" She asked.

"I want to, but I don't really trust anyone, especially with social services involved," Trisha admitted.

"Let's get a muffin; you don't want to go to PDMA hungry," She said walking with her into the kitchen.

Diana worked with Trisha in PDMA to try and help her connect to the severity of her situation, the one that had brought her to this place. Trisha insisted her accident was only a fender bender and that her child had not gotten hurt and that nobody had gotten hurt, so it was no big deal.

She had an opportunity to share from her own experience and said she knew how scary it was to face the fact that you put your child at risk due to your addiction.

When she saw Trisha roll her eyes, She had a flash of anger and said, “So, how did it feel when you were arrested and they took your son away?”

Trisha shot her a vicious look and got up to leave.

Diana in her gentle-but-powerful way asked Trisha to sit back down and answer the question. Trisha then cried for five minutes before she could breathe enough to talk about the horror of the police trying to put her son in a car seat while he screamed for her.

She was sitting on the front porch with Trisha when her boyfriend, Dave, got dropped off by the staff at the men’s program. He was handsome and had clearly tried to look his best for the visit.

She could sense Trisha's nervousness, as she squeezed her hand tight, as well as his nervousness despite his friendly vibe. Judy came out to the porch, welcomed him, and invited Trisha and Dave to walk over to Diana’s office. Word must have spread that he was here because a group of women came up from the backyard to check him out.

“Can you come with me?” Trisha said suddenly, gripping her hand.

“Sure,” She replied, “If it's okay with Diana.”

Trisha walked into Diana’s office who was already in full swing, chatting and laughing with Dave. She leaned over and asked Diana if She could come in with her. Diana nodded and said it was okay, if Dave felt okay with it. Dave agreed, seeming to note Trisha's nervousness. They all settled into their seats.

Dave cleared his throat and started in, “I want to clear the air.” He went on to spill the ugly details of the past two years of their drug use and drinking. “We tried to do the right thing; do things on our own; we thought we were smarter than our addiction and recovery. Until it all crashed down.” Dave admitted.

Sitting amongst the wreckage of the truth it was apparent that Trisha was having trouble breathing.

"Anything you want to add?" Diana asked Trisha.

Trisha couldn't lift her head, numb and buried by an avalanche of shame, unable to find words that mattered at this point.

Dave leaned in close and took Trisha's hand, "I have learned that until we face the truth about our addiction, we cannot be fully in recovery and take care of our son."

Trisha lashed out, "You are not his mother. You did not give birth to Chase and then choose drinking over your child."

"I am not his mother," Dave quietly agreed. "But I am the father who did not protect him and keep him safe."

"Are you in recovery today?" Diana asked, looking at them both.

"Yes," they both replied humbly.

There was a knock on the door. When Diana opened it, two-year-old Chase ran into the office and jumped into Trisha's arms giggling while he showed her the stuffed lion Judy had given him.

She could see his innocence and joy washing away Trisha's shame as she stood up and leaned into Dave. Dave put his arms around Trisha and Chase both.

A moment later, She watched as Dave, Trisha, and Chase hugged goodbye on the front porch.

"Why are there always so many feelings at once?" She wondered aloud.

"What's that?" Diana asked.

"They look like such a happy little family. My heart overflows for them and yet breaks for my own family; it's so intense."

Diana got up and looked out the window, "Pray; it's the strongest thing we can do. Prayer opens doors within us and around us."

She couldn't help but feel jealous that Dave was a good guy doing the right thing. For a split second, She thought about reaching back out to her ex, but didn't have enough denial left in her to even entertain the idea. She decided to do what the Buddhist monk talked about and lead with love and compassion.

Later, at dinner, She gave Trisha a hug. "I'm happy for you and your family.

I'm not gonna lie, I'm jealous that Dave is doing the right things and supporting you, showing up for his family. It gives me hope but also makes me face the reality that my daughter's father is not even trying to do the right thing."

"I know we have a long road ahead of us," Trisha admitted, "I was so afraid of facing the past, but now that it's all out, I can breathe and focus on the future, or as Diana says, *the now*." She paused, "Thank you for being so supportive."

Trisha asked to chair the meeting that night and talked about being a grateful recovery addict because for the first time she could trust that there was support and understanding here … and out there for her.

She had run out of cigarettes and decided to try and quit smoking. "There is no such thing as try," She whispered to herself walking out the front door after the meeting.

In health class, Counselor Maria challenged them every week to do at least one thing a day towards quitting smoking. She thought about *the now* that Trisha had mentioned earlier, and thought, *Why not become a non-smoker? Now!*

"Do, don't try," Maria would say, quoting Yoda, "Do or do not. There is no such thing as try."

She stood at the top of the wide stairs leading down to the backyard, watching everyone light up a cigarette below. They were giggling and talking, seeming so happy as they inhaled the cancer-causing smoke.

"Need a smoke?" Tara offered, holding out her pack.

"All set, thanks," She smiled, "I'm ready to cut down like Maria says." She was hesitant to admit she wanted to quit altogether.

She watched the smoke trail through the night air and disappear above Tara as she skipped down the stairs. *Strange*. She thought, *Am I looking at addiction?* It seems harmless, but it makes you sick. Everyone seems happy to be doing it, but you … cannot … stop.

She knew smoking was addictive, but had never really seen or thought of it this way.

Tired of looking at other people and wanting what they had, She tilted her head back, “I’m ready to be out of every trap!” She whispered it out loud to the million stars in the cold December sky, and hopefully to Dad and Grampy if they were listening and willing to help.

“Amen,” Big Sis boomed suddenly, wrapping her in a big hug.

“I didn't know you were behind me.” She jumped and laughed.

“I’m going to miss my Little Sis!” Big Sis smiled at her, “Keep the faith and keep walking the walk.”

“Who’s going to hug-bomb me when I least expect it?” She giggled, squeezing her Big Sis extra long.

“My sponsor is picking me up for the morning meeting tomorrow, then moving me to the sober house.” Big Sis said. “Waking up in a different place, but the routine stays the same.”

“Keep it simple. Seems simple enough,” She replied, then looked fondly at Big Sis. “You have been my anchor and my greatest cheerleader. I’ll call you when I get my phone tomorrow afternoon.”

Dear Emma, I miss you so much! One of my friends here had a visit with her family today, her little boy Chase made me think of you. I am sorry we can’t be together with Daddy and that he is not visiting you. Remember when I told you that I was sick and had to get better? Well, Daddy is sick too. No matter what, I know that he loves you more than anything; don’t ever forget that. I am meeting so many wonderful women and learning from each of their stories. I am realizing that we are all connected and all trying to figure out how to do our best, especially as mothers. I will always be there for you. That is what we are learning here: to be healthy and make good choices in the moment, in this day, and not worry about what is going to happen tomorrow. I quit smoking tonight, I hope you don’t remember me smoking, I know it is a bad thing and smells gross. I took a big step and wanted to share it. It’s weird and sad how companies make things that get people addicted. Today, I am doing the right thing. I am healthy. I am healing, and I am getting stronger. Love you to the moon and back, Mumma

Ghost

Now that She was a senior peer, she was allowed to attend Twelve Steps Community Meetings with sponsors and Everson alumni. Her sponsor had agreed to pick her up for the morning meeting. She was surprised at the swirling butterflies in her stomach. Even though Kate talked with her every day, it still felt like She was going out on an awkward first date.

"Don't worry, the first meeting is always the hardest," Kate offered, sensing her nervousness.

"Raise your hand and introduce yourself as a newcomer, it's important to let people know you."

She gripped her Styrofoam coffee cup even tighter and looked around. It was one thing to share at meetings in the house; but with a bunch of strangers and men, forget it. *Kate can't make me do it*, She thought, in an attempt to comfort herself.

Kate leaned over and whispered an encouragement, "When your heart is beating in your throat, you feel like you are going to throw up, and you are terrified to speak, that's a prompting from your Higher Power to do it. So that you don't have to keep feeling that way."

And then She did. *Hi, I am new ....*

Later, after she had shared, she felt like if she hadn't raised her hand, she might have become the-new-girl-who-puked-on-the-dude-in-front-of-her. It felt good when it was over.

She had said she was new, but didn't have to say she was an alcoholic or addict. Those old-fashioned labels still felt depressing and cult-like to her. Later, four women gave her their numbers at the break and said to call anytime for a ride to a meeting. They all seemed so comfortable talking to her.

After the break, a man behind her shared that he could not stop drinking no matter what he did. He shared, "I've been in recovery before and relapsed. I'm doing everything that worked back then. I have a sponsor. I'm going to meetings and doing service work, but I still can't stop drinking."

There was a haunting quiver to his voice She had never heard before. This man, this ghostly man, could not get out of the trap. She did not turn around to look at him but could feel his desperation in her gut. He was crying out for help that seemed beyond human rescue. At that moment, She prayed that a Higher Power – or maybe her own Grampy – would give this man the same kind of miracle that she had been granted – to stop drinking.

When the man finished sharing the group replied in unison, "Keep coming."

She wanted to snipe at this response but instead whispered it herself, "Keep coming." She knew there was hope here. It was odd, jumbled, smelled of cigarettes and bad coffee, but it was here.

An older woman named Trudy approached her in the parking lot, telling her how blessed She was to be at Everson. Trudy had not had the opportunity to go to treatment and had really struggled to maintain sobriety.

"I've been watching the women who come to this meeting from Everson. They have a spark about them, something special that's a real gift," Trudy said. "I see that spark in you too; hold on to it and keep doing everything you are doing."

"Thanks, that means a lot. Can I get your number?" She mumbled nervously.

"Of course, call me anytime," Trudy replied reassuringly.

"How did you like the meeting?" Kate asked.

"If you had told me that not only was I going to speak today, but that I would also be asking for someone's number, I would have told you I needed a new sponsor because you've lost it." She giggled.

She returned back to the house just in time for PMDA. When asked the daily "What's better?" question, She proudly replied, "I am sober and free!"

She couldn't think of a Challenge for the Day. She was stuck on processing all that had just happened at the meeting. She actually felt amazing after stumbling over her words, *I am new*. Plus, she got some phone numbers, saw a few cute guys, had real coffee, and prayed for the lost alcoholic in the back row.

"Are you open to feedback and suggestions from the room for your Challenge for the Day?" Diana asked.

"Yes, of course," She said confidently.

She was a senior peer now. She was pretty comfortable in PDMA and gave solid feedback to new women. A new woman, Sasha, who had been there only a week spoke up.

"You seem snobby and cliquish with some of the other women in the house and that makes me feel unwelcomed."

Diana corrected Sasha, "Nobody can *make* you feel something."

Sasha looked her in the eye, "It's like you think you're better than other people."

She was dumbstruck and wanted to say, *Who the fuck are you*? Instead, She just sat there silent. She had been so caught up with everything that she didn't look much past herself lately. She realized that when her own desperation lessened, her motivation to reach out to the new women had slipped. Sasha hit a sore spot. She heard the Buddhist monk's words coming back to her, telling her to build a space *between a reactive feeling and a response*. In that space between, there is power to decide how to respond.

She took a few long deep breaths before responding, "You don't know me and what I have been through and what I am still going through, but I am sorry if I have not been more welcoming to you."

She thought, *I've worked too hard to have some new chic call me out her first week. Why am I apologizing, for what, for working on myself? Screw her*. But none of that came out. It might have been the overwhelming compassion She'd felt for the ghostly man at the meeting, but She couldn't bear to hurt anyone today. She asked Sasha if she would walk the Grace Trail with her after lunch today and they could talk. Sasha looked shocked, looked over at

Diana, and just nodded. Her Challenge of the Day would be to open up to new people.

She met with the case manager that afternoon to talk about aftercare plans. Diana suggested a transition to a local sober house for at least a month after completing treatment. Social Services suggested 3-6 months before they would consider returning custody of Emma. She thought it would be easiest to just stay at Everson. Diana thought it would be helpful to go to a sober house for a month or two in order to build a network in the community, get a job, and learn to balance life in recovery out of the structured environment. This sounded reasonable, but She felt comfortable here and was secretly worried about the challenges in the *real world.* She stayed in touch with Big Sis and other women that were in sober houses and knew there was a lot of freedom. Many women had relapsed though. *I've got time*, She thought. She asked for a list of sober houses, but put it firmly on the back burner.

Walking the Grace Trail with Sasha was hysterical. Sasha was loud, clearly said what she thought, and brought fresh energy to the house. Sasha's personality matched her larger-than-life appearance: curly fire engine-red hair, polka dotted yoga pants two sizes too small, and a fleecy purple hoodie. Sasha didn't walk the trail; she stomped it. As much as Sasha had annoyed her at first, She admired her boldness.

"I might not seem like it, but I'm totally open to feedback," Sasha blurted out somewhere along the trail.

"That's helpful," She replied, "You sure don't hold back. I had to step back a minute in PDMA when you gave me that feedback."

"I've been told that before and I'm trying to work on not coming on so strong. My plan is to ask for feedback and suggestions tomorrow in PDMA. I come from a big family, so everyone was always talking over each other, and if you didn't yell, nobody heard you."

"This is my first time in treatment and I want to get it right, once and done," Sasha nodded vigorously, as she kept talking, "I am the seventh of nine children. Most of my siblings have addiction problems. I was adamant that I was not going down that road – in and out of treatment, homeless, and bringing babies into this mess. No offense." Sasha said.

T*here is something to be said for not holding back or getting stuck in your head,* She thought, as she listened to Sasha's tales of growing up running the streets in Southie.

Sasha's Challenge for the Day was to try yoga.

She agreed to go along with Sasha.

It was unusually warm outside so yoga was under the trees in the backyard. Being in nature seemed less scary for someone who had never thought about bending and stretching outside, or "being in your body," as the yoga teacher liked to say.

How can you not be in your body? She thought, but then again, she overthought most everything. The yoga teacher, Carmen, had a warm accent and everything she said sounded inviting.

"The ultimate goal of yoga is a sustained state of pure awareness and realization with the true or highest self. It is the art of being truly present in your body while connecting the soul and spirit." Carmen explained. With her soft curly black hair, flowered yoga pants, and flowy white shirt, Carmen was graceful as she bent and stretched.

Wait, She thought, *this feels like what the Buddhist monk and the energy healer talk about. Is it possible that this is all somehow connected?* They were taught to mindfully connect to their yoga poses while focusing on breath, balance, and presence.

"Each breath connects to the earth and to your higher selves," Carmen offered gently.

She had never experienced this connection to her limbs, her core, or her spirit. The final savasana pose was her favorite part – lying flat on the earth, on her yoga mat, under a beautiful tree whose limbs stretched in an expansive pose of their own. Carmen's voice drifted and blended with the swishing wind through the pine trees behind them.

She felt the tree was whispering a story to her about the creatures that lived high up in its branches. Grampy had taught her the difference between a bird chirp and a squirrel chirp which can be easily confused. The squirrels were busily collecting and storing up for the winter, chatting to each other. The woodland creatures had to learn to adapt and grow with nature and all seasons. They didn't fight against it or deny what was happening, try and control it, or punish themselves for not doing it perfectly. *Maybe they were onto something*, She thought. *Be more like the birds and squirrels.*

Sunday, at the Thought of the Day check-in meeting, someone announced that Anna had overdosed and died last night.

Her heart sank in sorrow for Anna who had left Everson after only a month. Anna had insisted she'd been in and out of these places for years and knew what to do when she had left treatment early, against counselor advice.

Sadly, She had lost count of the people she knew that had overdosed, but couldn't seem to shake her deep despair about Anna.

Before Everson, while She had been in active addiction, she would bounce between telling herself *it won't happen to me* and *I don't care if I die.* Now that life really meant something to her, losing someone she had known, really known – not like her so-called friends on the street – was different. She related to Anna, had understood her and wanted her to stay strong. What if Anna too really meant it, really wanted to be in recovery but slipped back? Reality seemed to be creeping in, too close for comfort. She had to believe that showing up and asking for help, actually helped. She closed her eyes, saying a prayer for Anna and for the ghostly man from the morning meeting.

Dear Emma, I love you! I really want to live and be the best I can be for myself and for you. I never thought about being alive as a choice before; it's really powerful to think about. You're so young now; but someday, when you are older, maybe you will read this and understand why we needed to be apart for a little while. A lot of difficulty is in life, but the best news is that you don't have to do it alone. Asking for help and giving support to other people makes you stronger in the best way. I choose life today. Can't wait to see you soon. Love, Mumma

Detour (20)

She was looking forward to phone time to listen to music and zone out under her favorite tree in the backyard. There was a text from the night before from a number She didn't recognize.

Hey, you looked hot at the meeting last night.

She felt creeped out but a little bit curious. She hadn't given her number to anyone nor talked to any boys. She texted back asking who it was.

Ryan. I was at the meeting with the guys last night and noticed you, I thought you noticed me.

He texted back saying he only had his phone for another half hour.

Want to meet up at the next morning meeting?

She had seen other women hook up with guys at meetings and had judged them harshly. She knew a new relationship was a mistake in early recovery. But oh, what a wonderful distraction from Anna's death and the grief and self-doubt that had taken over. *If I don't meet up with him, but just innocently text, it's not that bad,* She assured herself. They joked and flirted back and forth and suddenly it was time to turn her phone in. She reluctantly turned her phone into the office five minutes late. Staff warned her that being five minutes late would result in losing phone privileges the following day if it happened again.

She realized she had gotten so caught up with Ryan that she had forgotten to call her sponsor to confirm their weekly morning meeting.

During the Commitment Meeting that night, She was distracted, wondering which of the guys was Ryan. She asked around, targeting a few of the newer women who probably wouldn't try and talk her out of finding out about Ryan. One of the newer women, Kara, said she knew him from home and he had asked for her number too. Kara thought he had a girlfriend back home and that he had been at the men's program for a month.

Still convinced that it was innocent fun, She remained focused on finding out what he looked like. She didn't really plan to meet up with him but wanted to know who he was. He seemed nice enough in his text messages. The next morning, during PDMA check-in, She remembered that she hadn't written in her journal or prayed before bed for the first time in a while.

In group, Kara noticed. She commented with a smirk, "You seem distracted."

She ignored it.

"How are you feeling about Anna's death?" Diana turned her attention to her.

"It's sad," She said, pushing her feelings down. She'd rather think about Ryan.

She was looking forward to phone time again. Ryan had texted that he was going to get a burner phone dropped off to him so that they could keep in touch *when they felt like it*. He encouraged her to do the same.

During her visit with Emma on Monday, Sue informed her that she had spoken with Diana about Social Services approving a sober house within the next few weeks. Sue felt it would be beneficial for her to practice her recovery skills in an environment with less structure in order to further stabilize her recovery.

"Since this is your counselor's recommendation, it will also be the department's recommendation," Sue confirmed. "We want to see you learn to balance work, meetings, and recovery outside of treatment prior to your custody hearing in two months."

"Okay," She said, unsure of this plan.

She realized if she left early that she would have more freedom, be able to go to meetings daily, and hang out with her new sober friends, including Ryan. It would be nice to have visitation with Emma at the playground instead of at the house.

She was able to get a ride to the next morning meeting, telling Diana that her sponsor was out of town and that her sponsor's sponsor would be picking her up. Not really a lie, since her sponsor did technically live in the next town over. She tried to convince herself. She worked hard to believe her own lie. She was excited and anxious about meeting Ryan in person. Halfway through the meeting, She met Ryan at the dumpster behind the church. They had been texting for a week and She felt like she already knew him. He was shorter than expected for such a big personality, but cute. She leaned in to hug him and he tried to kiss her.

She stepped back in surprise.

"Everyone hugs and since we know each other, it's no big deal." He shrugged.

They spent the rest of the hour talking and when the meeting was over, she kissed him after all. She wanted to write in her journal that night about Ryan, but was afraid somebody might read it. She hadn't had a real secret since being at Everson and it felt both good and gross. She felt a twinge about checking in during PDMA. Seemed better to skip journaling all together. She was trying to hold on to shreds of honesty but they were slowly slipping away. She didn't even notice that she didn't write to Emma that night.

She was first in line for phone time and ran to the backyard to stoke the fires of her new spark with Ryan. That morning, Ryan hadn't texted her. She began texting him, over and over. She had never talked on the phone with him, but out of desperation she resorted to calling him. It rang twice then went to voicemail, which meant he *sent* her to voicemail. Her sponsor called. She annoyingly texted back saying she was waiting on an important call from her Mom.

Lies.

Her sponsor responded, *Call today if you still want a sponsor.*

She hadn't contacted her in almost a week. She didn't want to lie to her sponsor about why she hadn't called, so she just continued avoiding her. She only had ten more minutes of phone time to wait for Ryan's text.

At 5:10 pm, staff hollered, "You're ten minutes late turning your phone in and will lose privileges tomorrow."

She came in, dropped her phone in the main office, slammed the door, and ran to her room, pacing back and forth. Maybe Ryan was right and she should just get a burner phone so they could keep in touch whenever. She could not think straight and was angry that he had blown her off. She needed him to text her to make sure that their kiss was okay. RA Shirley knocked and then opened the door to tell her it was dinner time.

"What's wrong?" Shirley asked when she saw her pacing.

She wanted to scream and tell Shirley how freaked out she was that Ryan had blown her off. Maybe he didn't like her after all or didn't like the kiss. She felt like an idiot, a teenager; worse, she felt like she had during her active addiction: pacing back and forth, obsessing, not okay.

Holy shit, one tiny little lie multiplied, grew, morphed and took over. She thought, feeling lost and confused, lonely and stupid. It has only been one day that he hasn't responded; her mind countered, trying to override common sense. Maybe he got caught with the extra phone and they took it away or kicked him out. She tried convincing herself that he really did like her. They had so much in common and he did kiss her.

It doesn't matter what you're telling yourself. She could hear Big Sis's voice in her head. *What matters is how this is affecting you, acting like you did when you couldn't get drugs.*

Her hand shot up in PDMA the next morning when Diana asked if there were any burning desire check-in's. She was terrified that the sneaky demon that had awoken through a few seemingly innocent lies had somehow taken over.

"I met a guy at a meeting this morning." She spilled, "Then one thing, and one lie led to another. It's been a nightmare."

With her head hung low, she continued, "I was literally willing to lose my sponsor. I was distracted during my visit with Emma last week. I stopped journaling and praying, and I wanted to leave early so that I could hang out with whoever I wanted."

"What has been the most challenging part of this?" Diana asked.

"Lying to everyone, and actually, lying to myself," She admitted quietly.

After thinking about it, She realized that learning to deal with her emotions without self-destructing had taken the most work. Other women shared about relationships being a huge trigger for relapse for them in the past.

"Do you want feedback?" Beth, another woman in the group, asked.

She nodded, head down.

"I've always left treatment for a guy. The guy that was supposed to take care of me last time, we were supposed to help each other stay sober. Until one of us had a bad day and took it out on the other person." Beth shared, "I would end up believing that if we weren't okay, then I wasn't okay. I wound up giving up. It was like my recovery stability was directly tied to the stability of the relationship."

"I'm terrified of raising Emma alone," She admitted, breaking down into tears, "It took all I had to cut ties with Emma's Dad and let go of that fantasy. Who is going to want to be with someone with a kid?"

"You deserve to show up for yourself," Beth affirmed. "And to trust that you'll be happy."

She used Diana's office phone to call her sponsor Kate, apologize for blowing her off and told her about the shitty choices she had made over the past week, which seemed like a year.

"You are going to do what you do. I'm just here to support you if and when you want help," Kate said matter-of-factly.

"Thanks. I'll call tomorrow if I get my cell phone," She replied, annoyed by Kate's response, cutting the call short.

"It seems like Kate has great boundaries," Diana said.

"I didn't know boundaries made you rude," She replied, knowing Diana would *reframe* as she always did.

"Is there anything Kate could have done to stop you from getting involved with Ryan if you weren't willing to tell her the truth about it when it was happening?"

As it always did, the responsibility landed firmly in her lap. "Yup, it's me," She mumbled.

In her Diana way, she asked, "Isn't that good? If the blame was on someone else, you'd have no ability to change the outcome."

"I know, I know, if you're the problem, then you're the answer," She chimed in.

Her brain hurt, but She did like thinking for herself and not being blamed or told what to do and how to think.

"Thanks, Diana," She relented.

She called Kate back and asked if she would take her to a women's meeting this week. She blocked Ryan's number and told Kate the whole ugly story.

Later, She stood at the window watching the trees blowing in the wind and remembered what the energy healers had said about negative emotions having an important purpose of showing us where we are out of alignment with our higher self and true nature. She took comfort in the swaying trees and tried to breathe through her panic. Pulling out her journal, She looked back over her notes from the energy healing session in hopes of reclaiming how good she had felt. She had written about the shift and made a commitment to herself to remember how it felt to be bathed in light. She picked up her favorite pen and wrote about the feelings of being out of control. Five pages later, She saw it all with clarity, with deepest gratitude.

Dear Emma, whew, I am tired, but I love you more than ever! It's been a rough week. My counselor says that learning and growth don't go in a straight line; it is like a spiral. You go around and feel like you learned something, then before you know it you seem like you are back at the same spot; but you are higher up on the spiral, still growing. I guess it helps to realize there is no finish line; life is a process and we don't have to figure it out alone. I lost a friend that I met here. I am sad about it. I really get to know so many women here. We live together and see each other every day. I learn something from all of them. Even the women whose stories I hear, but don't keep in touch with help me learn about recovery. You and me, we are going to learn about and enjoy life, together, one day at a time.

Love you to the moon and back, Mumma

Acceptance

Humility had been the topic of a few groups that week and, ironically, She prided herself on what she had learned about humility. The way she felt now had to be humility, or was it humiliated?

During the Building Recovery Group, Amelia asked, "What does the word humility mean to you in recovery?"

She used to be annoyed at Amelia's stoic approach to groups, but had grown to appreciate the way that she asked questions without any judgment. She noted that she had become less emotionally reactive and defensive in groups and gave herself a silent pat on the back.

"I have a quiet, open awareness and desire for help," She replied with confidence.

She knew she needed to be honest on all fronts, willing to learn and listen. Remembering the desperation of her *near miss* – being willing to sneak in a phone and risk being kicked out of the program. Lying and manipulating had brought her to her knees. She would not make the same mistake. She continued to write about what she called an emotional relapse in great detail, about fooling herself and risking it all. She thought of the ghost man from the meeting who would have given anything to escape the grips of his addiction, but was lost wandering in elusive circles. He was a haunting reminder of the elusive trap of addiction. She knew that no matter what, she never wanted to go back to being stuck with only bad choices in front of her, driven by the compulsion to keep using, drinking, running.

Mothers at Everson had lost custody of their children because they had chosen a guy, stopped putting their recovery first, and turned back to addiction. *Love? Was it for love or fear of being with self? Or was it just another form of addiction?*

She became obsessed with the word addiction and asked Amelia to please look up the official dictionary definition. Googling the word addiction, Amelia read its crap description about addiction being a treatable, chronic medical disease involving complex interactions among brain circuits, genetics, and the environment.

"Blah, blah, blah," She scowled. "I want to know why good people risk and lose it all when they know better. Women do amazing work in treatment, have all the support in place, then relapse, lose it all, and die!"

"Dictionary.com," She asked Amelia to look it up again.

Amelia read the result aloud. "Addiction. Number one, the state of being compulsively committed to a habit or practice or something that is psychologically or physically habit forming to such an extent that its cessation causes severe trauma. Number two, physically or mentally dependent on a particular substance or habit, and unable to stop without incurring adverse effects."

Amelia looked up from reading. Everyone was dead silent.

"That's it." She shouted. "I am not going to die from this *addiction*."

She felt the surrender.

She got special permission to attend the Friday afternoon women's meeting. Kate picked her up early and talked about starting the Twelve Steps of recovery. She'd been to the step education meeting in the house and knew it was a thing, but had not really given much thought to formally doing the steps, whatever it meant. Kate talked about the steps as the actual route to being *in* recovery and not just being abstinent from substances. She heard someone at a meeting refer to the Twelves Steps as a process that changed everything but your name. She wanted to tell someone that was a turn-off and a reason for her *not* wanting to do the steps. She liked to think about running up and down the long steps to the backyard when she heard people drone on about the Twelve Steps. But, as typically happened lately, this other part of her seemed to step in and override her negative streak.

Maybe it helps to visualize walking up the steps, rising higher as I climb, above the past, above addiction, and into recovery.

"Maybe I'll go to a step meeting someday," She told Kate.

"You already are," Kate replied. "We are on our way to a step meeting now."

"Tricked again," She grumbled to herself, then took a deep breath and strapped herself into the ongoing rollercoaster of early recovery.

"We are on Step 1 today," Kate said, while walking through the church parking lot. "It will be a good first step meeting for you."

The old church smelled of wood and incense like they all do. She had been raised Catholic and had a soft spot for the traditions, stained glass, giant crosses, hard wooden pews and prayers. She took comfort in the memories but was surely not comfortable with the whole religion thing. She smiled thinking of the numerous times a day things could be both comforting and terrifying, happy and sad, good and bad.

At the meeting, an older dude named Grant talked about learning to live with life's paradoxes in order to stay sober. One of the main reasons he drank was because he didn't know how to handle feeling multiple contrary feelings at once, all the time in early recovery, and in life. He said he sometimes wanted simplicity and predictability, which he found in the low-bottomed existence of his alcoholism, yet he sat in meetings so calm and accepting of the upside-down-ness of life's inescapable paradoxes.

The meeting was in the room at the back of the church where they taught catechism classes. It brought visceral memories back – especially trying to memorize The Lord's Prayer – which is coincidentally how they close most AA meetings. Maybe it was a bit of foreshadowing that She would need that prayer. She was relieved they were not sitting in a circle and noticed that she was the youngest woman in the room by at least 20 years. She loved the older women at Everson, so for once, she was actually comfortable in a new meeting. She was amazed that Rachel, the woman chairing the meeting, had been sober for 25 years and still seemed to have an emotional connection to the story that brought her to AA.

"Recovery is a way of life, second to none," Rachel said. "I need to keep sharing my experience, strength, and hope in order to keep what was so freely given to me."

Hearing about strength and hope gave her something to hang onto. This is exactly what the women were doing at Everson at Commitment Meetings, night after night. She had heard some of them talking about *giving it away to keep it,* but had not really understood. It made sense now.

After Rachel shared, they started reading Step 1. "We were powerless over alcohol and our lives had become unmanageable."

She felt a pang of relief. She had hated the word *powerless,* and thought it was a cop out; but clearly the chaos that happened every time she had picked up alcohol had proved she was powerless over it. Day after day, She would promise herself she was not going to drink, and day after day, she would break that promise. Alcohol had taken over; drugs had taken over. She was not powerless as a person, but she had felt powerless over it. That made sense.

"I'll take you through Steps 1, 2, and 3." Kate informed her, handing her a Step Book, and a Step 1 Packet. She felt grown up and part of something different and real.

They drove back the long way, past the beach, having quiet moments of real gratitude. Nothing on the outside of her life had really changed. Things were still a mess, but She felt better. She liked women's step meetings and asked Kate if they could go back next Friday.

Prior to the Ryan incident, She had told herself she was fine being alone, with herself, single. Insecure skeletons were just inside the closet door waiting to come out and dance with her addiction. Small but loud voices of shame, doubt, and the dreaded codependency - *if we are not okay, I am not okay.* It was the master lie, a woman's Achilles heel. She pulled out her timeline from her Building History folder and reread it, realizing she had never not been in a relationship, starting at 14-years-old with her first boyfriend! Technically, She was not in a relationship right now, though her ever-growing conscience crept in to remind her that she was still holding on secretly to the distant fantasy of *maybe someday with Josh.* After all, he was Emma's father and if he ever got his shit together they could be a family.

During the Seeking Safety Group, Counselor Bethany pushed Jen hard to realize the fairy tale reservation she had about her abusive ex-boyfriend.

"It was my fault that my boyfriend got mad at me. After he hit me, he was always sorry and very loving and would buy flowers," a woman named Jen shared.

"Were there ever other times he bought you flowers?" Bethany asked gently.

"No," Jen admitted sadly.

Bethany talked about the cycle of abuse and finding worth in unsafe abusive places, which then becomes a habit, or addiction for the victim.

"Whether physical or emotional abuse, it can slowly become a pattern that seems normal. It's tough for women to identify or break out of," Bethany explained.

Bethany suggested Jen speak with the Domestic Violence Counselor that meets with women on Tuesday afternoons.

"I've always been in one kind of unhealthy relationship or another and have no idea who I am outside of that, it's terrifying," Jen admitted.

She felt badly for Jen but wanted to keep distance from this topic; it meant she had to let go of her own fantasy. Maybe She would talk to Diana about it, maybe she would journal. She would definitely pass when her turn came. Bethany told her She could not pass in this group. *Not sure who Bethany thinks she is*, She thought as she sat quietly. Bethany reminded the group that recovery is about gaining awareness and developing healthy boundaries and habits in all areas of life, not just abstaining from substances.

She quietly stewed for a minute, wondering if Bethany had ever been in an abusive relationship. Bethany seemed so strong and confident, her long black hair pulled back tightly, exposing her big brown eyes and long fake lashes. Yet there was something vulnerable about her too, like She related to the women as she invited the women to really go deeper and get more honest.

With only a few minutes left in the group, She finally admitted, "I can relate to Jen. I don't know how to *not* be in a relationship, even if it is a complete fantasy."

"Thank you for your honesty," Bethany said gently, nodding her head. "Be sure to talk to Diana about that during your next session."

She asked Judy if she could chair the nightly meeting, thinking about strength and hope. She opened up and talked about what true honesty with self means. She knew it didn't matter if we fooled other people. "If I'm fooling myself, I won't recover."

"How am I supposed to ever care enough about myself after everything I have done in active addiction?" Terry spoke up, timidly.

"A few months ago I felt the same way," She offered.

"Do you believe that I care about myself enough to do the work?" She asked.

"Yes," Terry answered.

"All you have to do is believe that I believe it's possible. That sitting in these chairs and showing up is a huge step in caring about ourselves enough to begin to recover."

She saw the doubt on Terry's face, remembering her own first week when she felt the same.

Reflecting, She shared, "The only real reason I came to treatment this time was to get my daughter back. I had completely lost myself and honestly didn't care if I lived or died. I would like to say I'm putting myself and my recovery first today, but I am not totally there. My daughter still comes first, but I'm making progress. I don't hate myself anymore and do believe I deserve a better life."

She thought about the steps she took – both big and small – to reach the point where she didn't feel hopeless and miserable. "Diana suggested I write a gratitude list. It seemed silly to me, but since I was miserable anyways, I tried it. Slowly, I started feeling less anxious. Simply writing the things I was grateful for became a positive new habit."

She took an extra-long moment of silence to end the meeting that night, a moment, a crossroads between the wreckage of the past and the possibility of a new start. Somehow the clarity of what brought her here, to the mansion by the sea – overflowing with women, pain, and healing – was clearing a path forward, to Emma and to herself.

Dear Emma, I miss you! I know how much we love the holiday season, starting with apple picking, hay rides, trick or treating, decorating the tree, making your list for Santa, and hot cocoa by the fire. I can't wait to do all of these things next year. By being away from each other right now, I am doing the work so that we never have to be apart for the holiday again. I am learning a lot about gratitude, which is a way of being thankful by focusing on what is good in your life.

Here is today's gratitude list:
Emma!
Recovery
Diana
My sponsor Kate
Blueberry pancakes
My single room
Feeling healthy
Judy
Falling Leaves
A warm winter coat
Emma!!

As always, my sweet girl, you are on my gratitude list twice. Let's make gratitude lists every day when I get home. Love you to the moon and back, Mumma

Sisters

Family visit days were usually pretty boring since it was a three-hour drive for her family

and they had weekend visits with Emma. That weekend her sister, Brenda, made a surprise visit. Brenda had contacted Diana and asked to surprise her, worried She might decline the visit. She was shocked when Brenda walked into the dining room, a visibly worried look on her face.

After small talk about college, Brenda broke down, "I blacked out at a party after drinking too many mixed drinks. I swore I wouldn't drink again, but felt so ashamed about not remembering what I had done, so I drank the next day. I swore I wouldn't turn out like you, and didn't know who to talk to about it, no offense," Brenda admitted, looking up embarrassed.

She reached over and hugged her sister, not remembering the last time they hugged. She remembered how good her sister always smelled and was surprised at the faint smell of cigarette smoke in her hair.

"It's going to be okay," She assured Brenda. "I'm so glad you are telling me; there is so much wonderful help you can access."

"I'm not saying I need the kind of *help* you need," Brenda said, pulling away, straightening out her jacket and sniffling as if to take back what she had said.

"I'm not saying you have a problem. I'm just saying if I'd been able to talk to someone in the beginning – before things got really bad – things might have turned out differently."

"I know," Brenda mumbled. "Drinking helps me deal with stress and pressure, but now it is causing me stress and pressure. How did you know you had a problem?"

"Hmm, I was so deep in denial and blaming everyone else I didn't think it really hit me until I had been here a few weeks. I know that seems strange, being in treatment and not realizing you have a problem. I see other women arriving here. Their lives are completely destroyed by drugs and alcohol, and they don't see the problem right away."

"How is that possible?" Brenda asked.

"I think when I first lost Emma, if I had fully faced that my choices got me here, I wouldn't have made it. I had no belief or hope that I could get better, so taking responsibility was too painful. Denial kind of kept me numb, then little by little, with the help of others, I was able to thaw out. It was like I felt a tiny bit better physically, which led to my mind feeling better. Connecting with other women was the beginning of my spiritual healing. I know it doesn't seem to make sense. I know now why they say *you can't do it alone."*

"Wow," Brenda said, putting her hand on her knee. "I had no idea. I'm so glad you have a support system."

"Have you ever thought about talking to a counselor?" She asked.

"I've been afraid to," Brenda admitted. "I've always kept stressful things locked up and tucked away so they don't bother me."

"Secrets keep you sick is what I have heard," She offered. "There is this really cool thing I learned about facing the past and being really present in this day. Kind of like every day is a clean slate, like a do-over. It's not perfect and, of course, I still struggle and beat myself up sometimes; but it helps."

She paused for a moment, looking around the living room at the families that were visiting. She recognized fear, anger, confusion, love, and relief in the faces of the mothers, fathers, grandparents and children of her Everson sisters. *We are all so brave*, She thought, *gathered here together piecing our lives back together, one word, one action at a time.*

"There's a free counseling service at school," Brenda shared. "I guess it wouldn't hurt to try it."

"I'm so proud of you," She said smiling. "You could also come to an AA meeting with me once I go to the sober house. Just to check it out."

"We'll see." Brenda grimaced.

Brenda had a lot of questions and they talked for an hour about parts of their childhoods they had never talked about before. Brenda had been so angry at her sister, thinking She could just stop using drugs, convinced she was doing it on purpose. Brenda saw other young women at the house and commented on how normal they looked and she couldn't believe they were addicts. She admitted she'd always had this stereotype in mind and realized that nobody plans on ending up in rehab.

"I've learned so much about myself and have actually been able to start choosing the kind of person, the kind of mother I want to be," She said proudly. "It's so much more than stopping using drugs and alcohol, it's changing everything else too, but in a good way."

Brenda looked at her with a curious smile, "I'm not sure what it is exactly, but there is something really different about you."

She explained a typical day in treatment to Brenda. "We are basically in different groups all day, working on ourselves. We have fun too; I've never laughed so hard as I have with these women. It feels good."

Brenda nodded her head back and forth, "Yeah, that's not really it. It's a feeling I get, a vibe that's different about you. It's a good thing."

The sisters made a pact to keep in touch now that they had connected for the first time, to talk about real things.

"Nobody in our family ever talks about real things ... unless there is a crisis," Brenda said with a smirk. "I sort of tried talking to Mom about things I was going through, but she minimized things and just brushed it off. You know how Mom changes the subject to something about her, then switches to her concerns for you."

"I know, it's hard not to take it personal when Mom doesn't listen and makes it about her," She related.

"I guess I was never able to talk to our parents. I get why drinking made sense to turn it all off," Brenda concluded.

"My counselor says people don't relapse because of situations, but because they don't know how to manage their feelings about situations," She shared.

"In addition to the PDMA group where you check-in with how you are feeling, I talk to my sponsor almost every day about how I'm feeling. Talking really helps manage the anxiety I used to feel, keeping everything bottled up."

Brenda seemed sad, "I'm kind of jealous that you have so much support. Must be nice."

"I am just learning to deal with Life on life's terms, and will happily be a support for my little sister anytime," She said, hugging Brenda and whispering, "Now let's talk about your new smoking habit!"

Brenda pulled away.

"I get it, " She said. "Smoking helped me deal with stress and anxiety. It seemed harmless. I get it. I was able to white-knuckle it and not drink during my pregnancy, but I still snuck cigarettes and felt horrible about it. I got the courage to quit a couple of weeks ago and have realized smoking was blocking me from dealing with things too. When I was stressed, angry, or anxious I *needed* to smoke. It's an addiction; that's how addiction works. It was stressful at times when I quit, but I knew it was a Band-Aid. When the intense cravings and emotions came up, it was a chance to process the real feelings I had been stuffing down by reaching for a smoke. I did a lot of walking, talking, journaling, and praying. I'm here to support you, if you ever want to talk about quitting".

"Thanks," Brenda whispered, stepping back into the hug.

She chose to not go out to a community meeting that night, wanting to spend her remaining days connecting with the house women who had become family. She looked back in her journal to the rantings of the scared angry woman she had been, who wanted to blame everyone else for her problems. *How sad would it be if it was everyone else's fault, then they would have to be the ones fixing it. Taking responsibility is actually empowering,* She thought.

An older man at the morning meeting always said, "The good news is because I'm the problem, I am also the answer." Maybe he said that every time he spoke because it was so true. She thought about Anna and the fact that nobody could have stopped her from using that one last time, no matter how much they wanted to.

It was Anna's choice, Anna's last choice.

Choice was another word they talked a lot about in the Unity Group. In recovery, we have choices. Even if they are difficult choices, we have them. In active addiction, drugs and alcohol make the choices for us, and yes, we are powerless over them. In recovery, we are told we have power, the ability to make changes.

I have changed, She thought.

Big Sis, my counselor, and the house manager had often commented that they saw changes but She hadn't yet felt much different.

She could *feel* it now; she knew the feeling might come and go, but it was real.

Dear Emma, I miss you! I had a surprise visit from Auntie Brenda this weekend. I was nervous at first, but it was so wonderful reconnecting with her. I really missed my sister but I was afraid she would never forgive me for making such a mess. I'm learning that everyone goes through difficult times and struggles to manage emotions. There is so much focus on the outward things in life; everything we are taught in school is about what do you want to be but no real talk about emotional coping skills and the importance of real, honest support. In a weird way, I am grateful this all happened because it is teaching me a new way of life – an honest, connected way that I want to teach you. You will have a better life and not have the need to numb yourself like I did. Love you to the moon and back, Mumma

A Christmas Story

"Seems like a Christmas Miracle," Diana said. "Your social worker is really sweet to schedule your visit on Christmas Eve Day. Why don't you do your PDMA check-in first, so you can get things ready for the visit?"

"I can actually say I am grateful to be here," She shared. "I had to walk through a lot of fear, pain, anger, sadness, and confusion, hanging on by a thread some days, leaning on everyone here. That's what's better; thank you all for the support. It's unnatural to be away from your child on Christmas; but together we are all not only getting through it, we're making the best of it."

"Look Mumma, there's a mismus tree on the front porch!" Emma squealed.

She loved that Emma still couldn't say *Christmas* and knew they would always call it a "mismus" tree. They had their visit in the art room and made an ornament for the living room tree. After hanging it on the perfect branch, they lay under the tree and looked up at the lights.

"Can we get big lights for our tree next year?" Emma asked. "These are pretty."

"Of course! Now let's open presents! I called Santa and he said you could open my presents a day early."

Toys for Tots had delivered presents for the moms while Judy had supplied wrapping paper and bows. Emma wanted to stop and play with each of the toys after opening them. *She's so precious, an angel*, She thought as her heart overflowed.

"Now open this one. It's special. I made it for you," She said, handing her the last present.

"A book, a book," Emma yelled.

"Mumma wrote that for you, and my friend helped me draw the pictures."

"It's called *The Magic Tree*, about a little girl named Noel who is away from home and she finds a magic tree in the backyard that helps her feel better when she is scared."

"That's my middle name, Noel!" Emma shouted proudly.

"That's my magic tree there," She said, pointing to the big beech tree in the backyard. "When I feel sad or scared I sit under the tree and listen to the birds singing above."

"What about when you're happy?" Emma asked.

"Yes, I sit under the tree when I am happy too. In the story, the tree remembers the little girl's happiness and reminds her when she is sad that happiness will return. Magic trees are everywhere; you can pick one in your backyard and use it until we have our very own tree at home."

After reading the book together and bundling Emma up in her puffy winter coat, they walked to the blue minivan.

"Read every day and remember we will be together soon, my sweet Emma Noel."

There were no tears this time as She strapped Emma into the car seat – just lots of love and "Merry Mismus!" She gave the social worker a special stuffed monkey for Emma to open Christmas morning and thanked her for coming on Christmas Eve.

As She walked up the steps, her new Little Sis, Jamie, was standing on the porch yelling at Judy. Neither one of them had on a winter coat and it was freezing outside.

"Just leave me alone and give me my cell phone," Jamie yelled, stepping closer to Judy.

"You don't have to make an impulse decision based on a feeling," Judy calmly replied, pulling her pink cardigan sweater in around her.

"I've made up my mind; there's nothing anyone can say or do," Jamie replied.

"Let's go inside," She prompted, positioning herself between Jamie and Judy.

"I'm done talking, and tired of thinking. I need all of this to stop," Jamie insisted.

"What do you need to stop?" She asked.

"Forget it," Jamie said, walking down the steps and towards the road.

She ran down after her, reminding her she didn't have a coat or cell phone, but Jamie just kept walking.

"Come on in," Judy called to her. "You can't force anyone to do anything and it's freezing out here."

She walked back up the front stairs, turning to see Jamie disappear into the distance as the snow began to fall.

"As tough as it is to see someone make a decision you know is going to hurt them, we can't override free will," Judy said, shaking her head.

"But what happened? Jamie seemed to be doing so much better, setting boundaries with her boyfriend and opening up."

"Secrets keep you sick," Judy said. "There was a message on the office phone that he was on his way. Clearly Jamie was talkin' the talk, but not walkin' the walk with him."

"But she doesn't have a coat or phone. Shouldn't we go after her?" She asked.

"The harder you chase people, the faster they run," Judy replied. "Jamie knows the way back to Everson if she needs to turn around, on her terms, her choice."

She felt bad for Jamie, but didn't feel guilty. She knew Jamie had to make her own choices.

She said a prayer for Jamie that night and imagined her surrounded by healing white light. She remembered the words from "O Holy Night," grateful that she was now kneeling, not falling to her knees in prayer.

Dear Emma, I love you! What a wonderful treat seeing you today, the best present I could ever get is being with you on Christmas Eve. I loved watching you open your presents. I'll think of you reading The Magic Tree book every night before bed, and snuggling the special little stuffed monkey you'll open Christmas Morning. I have started writing again and it feels so good, like coming back to an important part of myself I lost in my addiction.

I am so grateful for the family that is taking care of you so that I can get better. I'm excited that you will get to be with Nana and Brenda tomorrow. They love you so much. One of my friends made a bad decision to leave today and it made me sad. I've felt like running away before and it was really challenging to stay and work through the feelings. That's probably the hardest thing I've had to do, learn to manage feelings without making decisions that only hurt me later on. It felt good today seeing my progress. I don't freak out when I'm sad or scared and I can be there to support other people when they are struggling. As we learn and grow, it's also fun to think about new traditions. Maybe we will put Christmas lights outside on our Magic Tree once I come home. I like making homemade ornaments too. I'm looking forward to Christmas morning and seeing the sparkly star ornament we made today and hung at the top of the Everson Mismus Tree.

Love you to the moon and back, Mumma

Unfolding

The energy healers came back for the second session that week, the familiar scent of sage warming the air in the house. Sitting in the room with the group, She realized she had so many questions about what energy healing actually was. When She got the first session she had just agreed out of hopelessness when she would try almost anything to feel better. Now, having felt the positive effects of the first session She was very curious and wanted to learn more. She asked Ariel the healer to please explain the basic idea behind what they do. She leaned in to listen, wanting to take notes and really understand what was happening for her.

"Sure thing," Ariel said and went back over the basics: "Energy healing can help heal the effects of physical and emotional traumas. Our energetic bodies are intertwined with our physical bodies. All the traumas we carry physically, emotionally, and psychologically impact the functionality of our energy systems and vice versa. To maintain vibrant health, the body needs its energies to have energetic space to flow freely through the body. When energies become blocked – because of traumas, toxins, prolonged stress and muscular constrictions –it creates disturbances in the energy flow in our bodies. This over time contributes to mental, emotional issues and/or ailments and physical disease."

"Wow, thank you," She said, drawn in as if could have listened all day to the story of energy, of us.

"Can everyone benefit?" She asked. "My sister is struggling and could really use it."

"Yes, everyone can benefit from Energy Healing." Ariel confirmed, "Whether you are struggling with mental or emotional difficulties, experiencing physical discomfort, or are looking to bring your mind, body, and spirit into alignment, or just know there is *something more*, you can benefit from our services. Energy Healing opens you to a deeper sense of ease, well-being and purpose, and brings you back to your true self."

She looked around the living room at the other women who were equally as mesmerized. She felt that Ariel was sharing something that we all somehow instinctively knew, a wisdom that was awakening. Ariel continued, "Working with our energy systems is very inclusive. There is often a misconception that you need to be spiritual in some way to be open and receptive to healing. Energy healing is readily available to everyone who is interested and willing to receive it. You don't need to be spiritual or hypersensitive to energies to benefit from an energy healing treatment. As humans, we all have an energetic body that needs to be balanced and taken care of regularly."

"During my family visit my mom told me I seemed more peaceful and asked what I had been doing," a woman named Sarah said. "When my mom said that, I immediately knew that it was the first energy healing session I got that made the difference. I felt an overall feeling knowing that I was going to be okay. Since then I have been motivated to do the things in recovery I had been resistant to doing."

She knew in that instant the *vibe* Brenda was talking about during their last visit was from the first energy healing session she got. Her hand hurt from frantically taking notes. She wanted to absorb and remember everything Ariel said so she could share it with Brenda.

During the check-in with the group, a woman named Jess said, "My anxiety has almost disappeared and I am sleeping through the night for the first time. But I am also experiencing negative emotions more intensely since the first session."

"The purpose of anger, or any *negative* emotion, is to alert us that we are out of alignment with ourselves and what is best for us." Jacob, the other healer explained, "It's an opportunity to look at where we need to make *decisions* that would be in our best interest and not just get angry or complain."

She thought about situations with her family and in the house and it all seemed to boil down to needing to stand up, speak up for herself, set boundaries, and be honest with the people in her life. It seemed overly simplified; if it were that simple why didn't people just speak up?

She thought of her Little Sis Amy and how timid and afraid she had been the day she arrived. She was surprised when Amy went from being shy to flipping out on someone who had moved her book bag in group. The times when She had been able to speak up for herself were challenging. It took courage to be honest about how She felt. For so long She felt vulnerable and unsafe letting people know how she really felt. She attended many Building Recovery Groups on boundaries and had learned about what healthy boundaries are and how to set them, but taking action in real time is different. During the Refusal Skills Group, the assignment was to role-play saying *no* to someone who was asking them to use or drink. She was shocked at how hard it was for everyone, and for herself. People struggled, making excuses – maybe later, not right now, I'm busy, I can't, and rarely just said the simple but not easy word, NO.

Other women shared their experiences since the first energy healing session: sleeping better, less anxiety, more peace, ability to remain calm in difficult situations, and an overall feeling of hope for the future. The energy healers spoke about our nature as a spark of divinity, that light work reconnects us to our original divine blueprint and sense of purpose.

"This next session will help you more fully engage with your individual purpose and bring more joy." Ariel said with a big smile.

During these past months, She hadn't thought much about her purpose. It seemed the only purpose was to get into recovery and practice new coping skills in order to stay in recovery. She wondered if this tied into the Fierce Recovery conversations they have in the Unity Group. *The director would ask the group what length they would go to in order to save their child, and immediately the women responded 'any length', without even thinking about it. The next part really sparked a fire in her. Then what length would you go to in order to protect your recovery? Anything? Without even thinking about it, yes. Now how do you get to that same commitment to yourself? This is your chance, your time, your purpose to fully commit to a life of purpose.* She remembered feeling strong and inspired making this connection, knowing she would truly do anything to protect Emma. I am making this commitment to protect my recovery, my life.

"Since the first session, I have felt a sense of hope I have never felt before, but it's kind of scary," Becky admitted during her check-in. "In a weird way, not having hope allowed me to not care about succeeding in recovery and not caring. Having hope now seems like a reason to keep trying, but now I have something to lose." Everyone could relate and supported Becky in allowing herself to see what else hope had in store for her.

The healers explained that the first session reconnected you to your spirit and the second to your soul. Like the first session, She stood for a while, then sat. Ariel's chanting during the session was warm and soothing. Maybe it was the earlier explanation that chanting was like a prayer that brings the powerful vibration of sound to the session that soothed her, or the beautiful mysterious Latin words that melted her. When the session ended, She didn't want to move or open her eyes. She felt the deepest connection to something inside and ached to stay in union with it.

"It's time for the next group to come in." Ariel whispered in her ear, "Go outside and meditate or journal about your experience."

She slowly got up, accepted the hug, and walked to her tree in the backyard. There, She wept gently until she drifted off to sleep. She dreamt she had a sweet baby girl; but it wasn't Emma, it was herself. She felt an overwhelming love for this baby and *as* this baby. She was wrapped in a golden blanket made of light and seemed to float between herself and the baby. She knew she would always be there for this baby and that nothing could come between them. She was home.

She waited excitedly for Diana to arrive the following morning, meeting her at her office door. Diana had given her an assignment to get a picture of herself as a young child in order to have a reference point for her innocence and joy. She thought it was silly, and was embarrassed to be afraid and didn't do it. She saw a tear through the warm smile of her counselor as she told her of the dream of the baby girl.

"I asked my Mom to send me a baby picture last night," She shared. "You've saved my life." Without thinking, She jumped up and hugged Diana. "Thank you for not letting me off easy and for always asking one more question, then one more, challenging me to go deeper than I thought I ever could. For shining a light and a mirror for me to recognize and value my own unique strengths and gifts. For never filling in the blanks for me, but encouraging me to find my own answers and develop my own ideas." She gushed.

Diana had always talked about how recovery skills, when practiced, will become natural healthy habits. She saw this in action and was glad she had gotten a *tough* counselor.

Dear Emma, I have so much to tell you, there are so many amazing ways to deal with things. I had no idea! Life is still life and can be confusing and hard at times, but I am learning how to handle things in a healthy way and to really start healing. I had no idea that I just didn't know how to handle life. And I know that you have been through some really hard things, and I am so sorry. I will be there, really be there to help you heal from things your Dad and I did that have hurt you. I cannot go back and change what happened, but I promise you things will get better.

I can't wait to see you next week! I am writing a story about a lady who was sick but getting better. Love you to the moon and back, Mumma

Oz

On Thursday, we watched the *Wizard of Oz* movie. It seemed odd but was a nice break from family dynamics or boundary discussions. The next morning after the PDMA group, Anne and Judy gathered everyone in the living room, which usually meant something serious.

"You have the rest of the day to write, cast, costume design, practice and present the *Wizard of Oz* play," Judy informed the group. "Everyone needs to participate either with the script, set design, costumes, makeup, producer, director, etc."

Grumbles, giggles, and questions started swirling.

"Just have fun." Anne suggested, "It doesn't have to relate to recovery; be creative and play!"

As the staff stepped out of the living room, sliding the big wooden door shut, someone shouted, "This must be a trick, everything in treatment has to do with addiction and recovery."

She played the Cowardly Lion, her favorite character in the movie since she was a kid. She discovered a true vulnerability in the role and understood how much courage it takes to be real and not cover her true self up with anger and blame. Dorothy, the Cowardly Lion, the Tin Man, and the Scarecrow were all people in recovery trying to make it to the program – or Oz – safely. Along the yellow brick road of recovery, they encountered the wicked witch/drug dealer and the flying monkeys/old friends in addiction trying to pull you down and out of recovery. In the movie, they even got knocked out in a poppy field, who knew! Glenda the Good Witch was the Higher Power who reminds us to stay on the yellow brook road of recovery.

Once Dorothy and her friends made it to Oz, they realized they had always had the ability to go home, to recover. Turns out the *Wizard of Oz* really *is* about recovery, recovering your courage, mind, and heart. It was the most fun She had ever had. *This was kind of amazing*, She thought during the final curtain call. The staff jumped to their feet to give a standing ovation. She looked around the room as they took their final bow, as laughter and tears flowed between the staff and residents, and felt the true miracle in that moment, closed her eyes and breathed it in.

It had been over a week since She'd heard from Brenda. Since the surprise visit, they had been talking a few times a week and stayed connected. She felt like her sister finally understood that her addiction was not something she was doing to the family; it was something that had slowly taken over her life. During their visit Brenda had confided in her about her own problem drinking and continued to reach out for support. Brenda said she didn't think she was an alcoholic, but was worried about the similarities with her sister's descent into addiction. Brenda started seeing a therapist and discovered that she'd been depressed and using anger to mask it.

She tried texting and calling Brenda for almost a week with no answer or response.

She didn't want to involve Mom and open a can of unnecessary worms, but as the days rolled on she became increasingly worried.

When She finally called Mom and asked if she had heard from Brenda, Mom paused for a long time and then said, "I was planning on coming in and meeting with you and Diana this week."

Her heart dropped into her stomach.

Mom began to cry, "Brenda is in intensive care; she took a handful of pills and drank a lot of alcohol, I wanted to tell you in person."

"When and why didn't you tell me?" She screamed as her body went numb.

Mom was sobbing, "It happened a couple of days ago and we didn't want to worry you or upset you until we knew everything."

Amidst the numbing confusion, She somehow regained composure, "You do know everything! Brenda tried to kill herself and you didn't tell me!"

"It was not a suicide attempt. She didn't leave a note." Mom insisted.

She knew this made no sense and suddenly realized her mother must be in shock. She wanted to throw the phone into the woods and somehow go back in time and be able to help her sister.

"Brenda is in a stable, yet high risk condition. She's out of the coma." Mom offered.

"Coma?" She gasped, "How could you not tell me my sister is in a coma?" Her head spun in helplessness.

"Can you call me back with Diana?" Mom asked.

"No, you have to tell me what happened and why, and how, and why, Mom, why?" She broke down in tears.

Judy heard her sobbing and went outside to check on her.

"I have to call you back. The doctor is here," Mom said, trying to catch her breath.

She lay crumpled on the ground in the backyard sobbing, a few women surrounding her.

When Judy arrived, she wrapped her arms around her and just kept saying, "It's going to be alright. You're not alone."

Later that afternoon, Diana brought her into the office to call her Mom. By that time, She was wiped out and had run out of tears. She was trying to focus on her sister and not her guilt. Maybe She should have told Mom about Brenda's drinking and depression. She knew Brenda had started therapy and said she was drinking less and feeling better, so how could she have known? *Who found her, how did they feel, what if they hadn't found her?* The dizzying questions just kept spinning around her.

"Brenda was moved out of ICU this afternoon and will be moved to a psychiatric stabilization facility once she's fully medically stabilized," Mom said calmly.

She needed and wanted to be mad at someone and Mom was as good as anyone else. She needed to stop blaming herself. Diana sensed her anger and motioned for her to stay calm and breathe.

"How could you have not known that things were so bad for your daughter?" She begged.

Mom was quiet, but She could hear her choking back tears.

"I'm sorry, Mom. I feel terrible for lashing out. I'm so freaked out and scared."

"It's going to be a long road for Brenda and we are going to have to be strong for her," Mom exhaled.

"We are going to have to be strong *with* her," She quietly said.

"Yes, that's what I meant, thank you," Mom accepted.

Diana sat with her in the stillness. There were no words for the layers and layers of shock, anger, grief, horror, pain, regret, and confusion. She sat looking out the window at her favorite tree in the backyard and wished for the innocence of this morning when the biggest problems she'd had now seemed miniscule. Her focus had been so completely on herself that She was not aware of the depths of struggle people in the real world were having.

"I feel frozen in fear for what could have happened, mixed with overwhelming amounts of gratitude that Brenda is alive."

"What have you done in the past when you felt completely overwhelmed with a mix of emotions?" Diana asked.

She was aggravated at the question and just wanted Diana to give her answers this one time, even though she knew there were no answers. She knew she would pray, long and hard and on her knees for her sister's recovery. *Recovery, huh, there's that word, it feels safe and hopeful when it is for someone else, someone you love.*

She wanted a million answers to a million questions. She needed something that would assure her she was not somehow responsible for all of this. She pulled out her journal that night and put pen to paper. *I just love you so much Brenda. I'm sorry, I'm so sorry.*

Emotionally strung out was her PDMA check-in. She felt ashamed and didn't know why and didn't want to talk about it. She just shrugged when Diana asked if She wanted to share. Most of the women in the group knew what had happened with Brenda. It felt like a betrayal talking about it. She had never known anyone who tried to or committed suicide. She felt weird and uncomfortable being so close to it now.

"Has anyone ever thought about opiate use as suicidal?" Diana asked, "The overdose rate is so high and the risk of getting a deadly synthetic drug even higher."

She thought back to her overdose last year after losing custody of Emma. She had never thought of it in terms of suicide since someone gave her Narcan and revived her. A chill ran up and down her spine as She connected the dots.

The thought of poor Brenda having to go through all of this was more than She could handle. I'll take the bullet for the family if I have to, She bargained with herself, but left Brenda alone. She left the group and walked the Grace Trail for over an hour, around and around, stomping, crying, praying, talking out loud and walking. Walking away, walking to, walking it off.

Let's see if they mean what they say, She thought as she marched to Anne's door, which actually was open. The sign on the program director's door said *extra help,* but She had always wondered if that was some sort of trick, never having the courage to ask. Today was the day. She asked to talk and shut the door behind her.

Getting right to the point, She asked, "What's the deal? It seems like you come into recovery and all hell breaks loose like some sort of cruel test from the universe."

"I am so sorry to hear about your sister," Anne said, nodding her head.

"Thank you," She said. "It's all a mess and I am tired of the mess."

She waited for some inspirational words at least.

"Yes, the human condition is a mess most of the time. Nobody tells us that, do they? We don't come into this life with instructions or explanations when things go terribly wrong."

"But it's not fair," She said. "How much is one person supposed to be able to handle, and don't give me that *God doesn't give us more than we can handle* crap."

Anne nodded, "Nobody has all of the answers, do they? The best we can do is keep showing up with courage and honesty and remain connected to a support network."

"But don't you get paid to have the answers?" She begged, "What kind of extra help is this?"

"If I had the answers, what would happen when you leave?" Anne calmly asked. "Together we figure it out, learn how to process and cope with the challenges, the pain."

She came into the office ready to argue and stomp her feet and didn't know what to do now.

"Sometimes it helps to yell, stomp your feet, slam a few doors and bring what is inside boldly out," Anne invited.

"How did you know that was my plan?" She laughed.

"This is real." Anne confirmed, "Treatment isn't a hideout for life's trials, it is a front row seat without buffers or excuses. You are courageous for showing up every day and facing the truth of life without apology or blame. In your strength and compassion for those that suffer, including your sister and mother, you are a leader, a truly powerful woman able to be there with, for, and beside people that need you."

"Thank you," She whispered. "I don't feel very strong."

"What have you learned about your strengths since being in the program?" Anne asked.

"Until the first time I met with Diana, I had never thought I was strong, at all. Sometimes I felt tough, when I needed to, but not strong. Now I know I have courage, I am kind, compassionate, and funny." She answered clearly.

Anne smiled, "You didn't even have to think about it when asked. That's strength."

"What else have you learned about yourself?" Anne asked.

"I've started writing again. I forgot how much I love writing. I always feel like I'm in a special kind of flow when I write. As far back as I can remember as a child, I have felt like I was meant to write."

"Creativity is the Creator's gift to us. Using our creativity is our gift back to the universe," Anne shared.

"The Creator, I like that; it's easier than the God of your understanding, as they say in AA," She replied, "I'm trying to figure out the whole spirituality thing."

"I believe our purpose is to remember that we are divine beings, learning to love and help each other," Anne shared. "I once read that, when we are born, our memory of being angels is erased. Our purpose in this world is to remember, reconnect, and share our divinity. I believe people with addiction don't have the knowledge of their divinity fully erased before birth. We know there is something missing, a spiritual connection, a spiritual community."

"Isn't that what religion tries to do?" She asked.

"Religion has very specific rules and doctrines, while spirituality is more of a search for peace and purpose, developing beliefs around the meaning of life and connection," Anne explained. "The connections made through the fellowship in Twelve Steps Meetings begin to heal the disconnect."

"Kind of like what you said in the Unity Group about the opposite of addiction is connection," She said.

"Yes, there is unconditional acceptance and support in Twelve Step programs that help people rediscover their own spiritual connection, through others. It's all related, and the connections you make with women in the house expand your sense of possibility. Healing communities restore our faith in ourselves through the honest touch points we have with each other.

"It's kind of like finding a new family," She realized.

"Yes, a soul family,' Anne said through a smile. "One with unconditional acceptance, just as we are."

Anne's words reached a place of knowing within her.

"Yes, thanks for talking, yes." She said, standing up, "It's wild how I thought coming here was about learning how to not to drink and use drugs, but it's really about learning, or re-learning how to live. Thank you, for everything."

At 3:00 pm, She called Kate and told her about her sister Brenda. Her sponsor had no great words of wisdom or guidance.

Kate just listened patiently, offering, "Brenda is lucky to have such a supportive sister. This is an opportunity for you to be a strong support for your sister and mother right now."

"How can I support my family while being so far away in treatment?" She asked.

"You *are* strong, by being open and honest about your feelings and learning healthy coping skills. That is what your family needs right now," Kate assured.

"I feel guilty for being the one that always needs help and attention, but I hear what you're saying, I *am* learning to handle things differently."

Kate shared about a tragedy her family went through last year and that during the panic and trauma of the event she was able to use her support network in the program and remain grounded for herself and her family."

"It doesn't matter how much time you have in recovery; we all only have this one day. Using the tools in real time will get you through *Life on life's terms*."

Kate always had this simple way of putting things that not only put her at ease, but gave her confidence and hope that she would be okay, no matter what.

She wished she had ruby slippers to click together. "There's no place like home." She mumbled to herself.

Dear Emma, I wish I could hug and squeeze you so tight right now! So many challenging things are happening, it's been a rough day. I'm so tired, but really glad I don't have to react and make decisions that aren't good for us. There is this saying people here use, Life on life's terms. It used to make me mad; but I get it now, we can't control anyone else's choices, all we can do is control our own reactions and choices. It is scary at first, feeling out of control; but they also tell us that we are not alone, there is always someone to talk to. Growing up, I never really had anyone to talk to about my feelings. I hope you know I will always be there to talk to you about your feelings, and we will keep learning together how to make the best choices for us. We had a fun day this week doing the Wizard of Oz as a play. I got to be the Cowardly Lion and it was amazing. I felt the desperation the lion had to have courage, realizing I am getting stronger every day.

Love you to the moon and back, Mumma

The Protector

She had contacted local sober houses trying to figure out which one would be best since her discharge date was coming up. Word was out about which houses were less strict and which were tough. She didn't even bother looking at the looser houses because she knew the accountability in the stricter house would give her a better chance at success. She kept in touch with Big Sis who was at one of the houses where there was a lot of turnover rumored to be due to relapses, and decided against that house.

She never thought she would stay on the Cape, but the recovery community was strong and her sponsor only lived a town over. She was relieved you could return to PDMA for the first two weeks after leaving as a step down. Being able to touch base in the morning with the group would be helpful during the transition. She settled on a strong sober house that had been around for a long time, and the manager was Everson alumni. It felt like solid accountability, as She heard Diana's voice in her head, *the strength of your recovery is the strength of your support system.*

Her mother continued to pressure her to find a sober house closer to home. This didn't make sense to her since Emma didn't live there and Social Services would continue bringing her to the Cape for visits. She figured Mom wanted her closer to home just to keep an eye on her and make sure she did the right thing. Mom watching over her never worked. Someone trying to control her, treating her like a failure waiting to happen had been a trigger for relapse in the past.

She had developed an identity separate from her family over the past months, one of a strong independent woman in recovery. She was no longer the fuck-up in the family, the scapegoat for her parent's unhappiness, or her mother's project. She felt torn because Brenda would be going home after she got out of the mental health stabilization program. But the closest sober house to her hometown was in an area where She had *used* and she didn't feel strong enough to see those people. She loved her family but with Diana's help she had to unlearn much of what she had learned growing up. The changes She had made were still very new and she didn't need pressure from her family on top of the challenges of the transition. Staff always said the healthy habits you developed would translate into healthy habits for life. The healthier habits and coping skills put in place in treatment, the better.

She was looking through her desk for a letter Brenda had written when She found her Myers Briggs Personality description: The Protector.

In the house meeting every week, Judy sent out a sign-up sheet for taking the Myers Briggs personality test which could help her understand her innate personality type, strengths, and weaknesses. Big Sis had encouraged her to take the test.

She read the results: *the INFJ-introverted, intuitive, feeling, and judging, or The Protector has strong capabilities, they trust their own instincts above all else. They can be perfectionists who doubt that they are living up to their full potential. They believe in constant growth, and don't often take time to revel in their accomplishments. INFJ is a natural nurturer; patient, devoted and protective.*

She felt a surge of pride and guilt rush over her, crashing like a wave on the shore. *Yes, I have always had strong instincts, high standards for myself, and have been a nurturing person, but addiction stole those things along with everything else*, She thought. She felt her head spinning and reached for her journal, asking the question over and over, *how she could not have known that her own sister was in such a dark and hopeless place.* She found herself writing about the energy healers' idea that we cannot step in between others' lessons and choices and take them on as our own. She knew her family couldn't have done that for her when She was spiraling no matter how they tried. I will protect and nurture Brenda in any way I can moving forward and I am committed to growth and learning, trusting my instincts. She wrote in big letters across the journal page. I Am in Recovery Today.

Dear Emma, my sweet Emma, did I ever tell you the story of the silly doctor telling me after two different ultrasound tests that you were a boy? What a wonderful surprise when you were born; we had to pick another name because Noah would not fit!! You were perfect, sweet, and loving from the minute I met you. I just want to be there for you, really be there for you to protect you. I know life will still be life and I cannot always protect you from getting hurt, but I can be there by your side with love and understanding, always. You remind me of Auntie Brenda in so many ways, like how when you make your mind up about something, there is no changing it, and what a good listener you are. I am excited for us to get closer to Auntie Brenda and maybe someday we can all share a cute little house, maybe near the ocean. I am getting stronger every day. I can feel it, especially through the challenges.

Love you to the moon and back, Mumma

Serenity

In PDMA, She made a commitment to write her mother a letter, thanking her for all of her support these last months. She wanted to explain why she needed to go to a sober house on the Cape after treatment. She sat down after dinner but couldn't get any further than Dear Mom. She wrote a few sentences, scratched them out, then a few more, getting more confused and uncertain. She shared about trying to write the letter in PDMA the next day.

During feedback, Jill shared, "Diana had me write an *as if* letter where you freely write whatever comes out for five minutes without worrying about the wording or thinking about how the other person might react. Once you write the letter, you can then decide what to do with it, send it, burn it, rewrite, etc. It helped me clarify what I wanted to say. It was weird, after writing the letter, it almost felt like I had worked through a lot of the issues through the writing."

That night the *as if letter* flew onto the pages. Love, anger, sadness, regret, rage, loneliness, gratitude, disappointment, and amends. Amends, She learned through the Twelve Steps Meetings means a change, not an apology. It refers to taking responsibility for having hurt someone and then making a change in behavior, not just apologizing. She had said sorry way too many times, but never made the changes. She wrote about her regrets having hurt her Mom, and the steps She was taking to change and not repeat those behaviors. She read the letter in PDMA the next day and felt the actual resolve of so many of the issues she thought she had with her Mom. Turns out they were mostly her issues.

"My Mom is doing the best she knows how to do with what she was taught," She realized. How strange recovery is, you get to stop and really look at life, choose what is working and what isn't, and get help changing."

"Sounds like the Serenity Prayer," Sam observed, then went on to recite it with pride. "God grant me the serenity to accept the things I cannot change, courage to change the things I can, and wisdom to know the difference."

Guilt still reared its ugly head now and then, like an old bad habit that had worked a groove in her mind. She'd been talking to Brenda every day and felt way less anxious about her part in the situation and her sister's wellbeing. She had yet to tell her how she felt but apologized for being selfish and self-centered. Maybe that's what She was feeling bad about. She wanted to talk to the Buddhist monk about it. He had talked about forgiveness as a form of *love*; not accepting what someone had done to hurt you, but loving them and freeing yourself energetically. She liked that idea and as much as She wanted her sister's forgiveness, She realized she needed to forgive her sister, to truly love her sister. It almost felt wrong to admit this to herself, but a relief at the same time.

The topic in health education that morning was healthy habits. Counselor Maria was always so excited about topics like smoking cessation and exercise. She knew they were in for a lively group. Maria asked people to shout out their current healthy habits: walking, going to the gym, decreasing or quitting smoking, eating healthier, praying, meditating, journaling, attending daily meetings, doing step work, calling sponsors and reaching out to new women. She was blown away because she had made every one of these a healthy habit! She wanted to remember how dreadful quitting smoking was so that she didn't ever start again. Maria asked everyone to raise their hands when she called each healthy habit out. She hadn't ever looked at it all in one place and felt pretty proud. One thing She had been resisting was meeting with a recovery coach. She didn't think she needed a babysitter when she left. Big Sis had been working with a recovery coach named Marissa and said she was a great support, so She finally agreed.

She noticed that Abby, one of the mothers in Maria's group, hardly raised her hand for anything. Baby Jackson had been pretty sick detoxing since birth and had to stay in the hospital. Jackson was reunited with Abby two weeks ago and she seemed to be struggling to get into a routine. Abby was so busy taking care of him that she couldn't prioritize her own self-care.

She approached Abby after the group and asked if she could babysit Jackson this afternoon so Abby could go to acupuncture in her place.

Abby declined, "Jackson is really fussy in the afternoon and I'm nervous about having anyone babysit him."

She noticed Abby's lower lip quivering as she picked at her pale dry face.

"I'll come over to the annex now and spend time with you and get to know what he needs," She offered.

Abby looked sad, asking, "Why would you want to give up acupuncture, for me?"

"People reached out a helping hand to me which helped me accept help, and I want to do the same thing for you," She said warmly, remembering how hard it was to believe or trust people in the beginning.

At 1:30 pm, She went to Abby's room to babysit. Abby was sitting on the bed crying and holding Jackson. The room was sparse, just a mirror on the wall and an open duffle bag filled with baby toys. It felt like Abby was half here.

"What's wrong?" She asked.

"I can't leave the baby." Abby broke down, "He's still sick a month after being born addicted. I did that to him! I can't bear the guilt. It's too heavy. How will I ever make it up to him?"

She reached out and put her hand on Abby's shoulder as she sat and wept with her crying baby.

Abby continued, "Why would you want to help me? I'm a monster. I can't selfishly do something good for myself while my innocent Jackson is suffering."

"Is that why you keep to yourself?" She asked quietly.

"I don't want the other women knowing what an awful Mom I am, blaming me for his tremors and discomfort." Abby confessed.

She felt at a loss for words and could only imagine how tortured Abby felt.

She hugged Abby asking, "Are you doing the right thing today? What do you have to be ashamed of today, just since you have gotten out of bed?"

Abby looked confused, "I am doing the right thing today, but I am afraid I will always be ashamed of what I have done to my son."

She leaned in closer, "Try really hard to just think about today. Are you a good mother *today?"*

Abby whispered "I am a good mother… today."

"Then give me that beautiful boy, get in the van, and go to acupuncture because a good mother takes care of herself. I'll help you unpack and set up Jackson's baby toys since you are both here to stay," She said with a smile.

Everson had a wonderful troop of volunteer babysitters from the community who came daily to take care of the babies while mothers went to groups. This gave the mothers a chance to be with their babies and still benefit from the full treatment program. Sometimes five or six women in a friend group would come in to babysit the babies and then all go out to lunch together. Most of them had grandchildren that lived far away and now their favorite part of the week was coming to Everson to hold the babies.

This afternoon, She enjoyed hanging out with just the mothers and their babies. Jackson started to fuss while drinking his bottle and one of the other mothers, Jess, knew just what to do to calm him down.

"Have you babysat Jackson before?" She asked.

"I haven't," Jess replied. "Abby keeps to herself, but I get it. My oldest daughter had NAS when she was born so I know what to do."

"Can I ask what NAS is?" She asked.

Wrapping Jackson snug in a blanket to help calm his tremors, Jen explained, "Some babies born addicted to drugs or maintenance medications suffer with neonatal abstinence syndrome. The poor little things can suffer symptoms for up to six months – tremors, stomach cramps, irritability. It's pretty sad, but there are ways to comfort them."

"Would you share that with Abby?" She suggested.

"Abby seems pretty shut down, but I will try and talk to her," Jen replied.

Just then a volunteer named Mary came in, bringing diapers and baby clothes. "Hi ladies, I am so happy to see you all here!" Mary squealed.

Mary beamed with light when she saw the room full of babies, stopping to play with each of them. She pulled a handful of small shiny pink stones out of her pocket asking each of the Moms to pick one. When she reached her, She waved away the stone and said, "I'm just babysitting while Abby is at acupuncture."

"There is no such thing as just babysitting! What wonderful support you are!" Mary insisted that She take a stone. "This is rose quartz which energetically helps with healing, opening the heart, and grounding." Mary explained, her eyes twinkling.

When she settled in with a baby in her arms, Mary shared how she had been the chairwoman of the board and how much her heart and soul was for the babies, the mothers in recovery, and for Everson. Mary's hope and joy was contagious. She shared how blessed she felt to have the opportunity to be a part of the baby's lives.

She asked Mary questions about the beautiful house they were in, so Mary told the story of the Friends of Everson. A local woman named Martha had noticed the women pushing babies in their carriages out in front of the old house some years ago, and had stopped in to see how she could help. Martha fell in love with the work being done with the women and babies and so she had gathered two of her friends to form the Friends of Everson.

"She noticed the old house could use much-needed restoration, so over the years they raised and donated money to restore the beautiful Victorian mansion so that women would have a beautiful place to restore their lives and their families." Mary beamed with joy as she shared the history of the house and the program. "It's second to none."

One of the mothers came in after her group meeting and gave Mary a big hug. She thanked her again for the beautiful gifts she had received at Christmas time. She shared with the group how Santa came for the Christmas party and took pictures with the babies. Everyone in the house got special Christmas bags full of new clothes and shiny things, all donated by the community. The volunteer babysitters had made up special bags for the mothers and babies, and their generosity was truly overwhelming. One of the volunteer babysitters, Rosemary, loved to squeeze the babies and say, "It takes a village of love, and we've got it."

She sat taking it all in – the Moms, the babies, Jackson, Mary. She felt such serenity in this room.

Dear Emma, I hope you are happy and somehow know that we will be together soon. I have been spending time with the babies here and remembering when you were a little baby. I can look at your baby pictures when I get my phone and it makes me so happy. I did my best to be a good Mom and be there for you when you needed me. What I am realizing is that you need me in so many different ways than I realized. I am starting to understand why people say they are grateful to be in recovery. It forces you to learn better ways to live and take care of your children.

Love you to the moon and back, Mumma

Self

She was feeling so good about herself lately that she asked for feedback in PDMA that morning.

A woman named Jackie asked her, point blank, "What's so hard about just being with yourself? You are always busy or hanging out with other people. It's like you're afraid to be alone."

The word *alone* smacked her in the face.

She wanted to snark back and say she was fine with being alone, but the truth was that she really had no idea. She felt herself spiraling and regretted asking for feedback. Diana said something, but She was already deep in the thesaurus of her mind.

Alone, She had to look up the word, *having no one else present, being on one's own. Didn't they always say in Twelve Steps Meetings that 'you are not alone?'* She wondered. *Okay, so give me a challenge,* She thought.

Being challenged was the whole goal of PDMA.

She got a computer pass and researched what people do when they are alone. She liked the idea of knitting or trying Qi Gong. Both of these were offered at the house. Her plan was to try both - she'd learn to knit with the volunteer knitters and attend the Qi Gong group, and then she'd try these activities *alone* in her single room. She would crush this *being alone* challenge.

All of her focus remained on not dropping a stitch that night when She was crocheting in her room. It felt easy being alone when her mind and hands were wrapped up in one piece of art. The next morning, She found a secluded spot in the side yard and practiced Qi Gong alone, slowly moving her energy up and down, in and out of her energy field. She felt very cool, being in her own world, practicing moving energy and being content.

She got a message that night – there was an open bed at her first choice sober house. The house manager wanted her to move in by the end of the week. She was excited and terrified at the same time, anxious to talk to Diana. She knew it was only a week before her discharge date so it was the right time.

She was unsure why she felt so nervous.

Later in PDMA, She got a lot of feedback about the work she had done and she was encouraged to keep doing the same routine when She left. She was reminded that the sober house would be structured and a strong support system would be there and in the community.

"What's your fear?" Diana asked.

She shrugged, not really knowing.

"Were you fearful coming into the house that first day?"

"I remember feeling really angry, but I know that was just a safe mask for my fear, my terror of where my life had ended up, without my daughter. So, yes." She paused. "I've worked so hard, but I've also seen other people who have worked just as hard and they relapsed anyway."

"Do you have any reservations?" Diana asked.

As many times as they had talked about people, places, and things that might be a trigger, or the fear that She would relapse if something bad happened, she was drawing a blank. She always thought if something ever happened to Emma, She would not be able to handle it. She heard people in meetings talk about getting through horrible tragedies and staying connected to their recovery network and staying sober.

"No, I don't have any reservations. If something happens, I've built a strong support network and will stay connected," She said with confidence.

"Hi, I'm Marissa," an enthusiastic woman announced, sliding into the seat next to her at lunch. "I'm your recovery coach. Great to meet you."

She looked around to be sure that Marissa was talking to her; but given how loud she was talking, it was hard to mistake.

"Diana said you wanted to meet. I hear you're getting ready to move on." Marissa's excitement distracted her from the urge to be annoyed.

"Diana doesn't miss anything," She joked.

"Coaching is an additional support for your recovery, especially during the transition out of treatment," Marissa explained while taking a french fry from her plate.

"How is it different from a sponsor? She asked.

"We'll keep in touch daily and meet up once a week. I can take you to meetings, help you make an action plan for things you need to get done, and help you stay accountable." Marissa explained, "Recovery can be fun! We can go running, join the softball team, go to the beach … you've gotta have fun!"

"Thanks," She replied. "You make it seem so normal."

"It is! We don't get sober to be miserable, right? Seeking out fun and growth opportunities is what I love helping people do. I'll pick you up for coffee and a walk tomorrow after the PDMA group."

Thursday morning, She got a message from Diana that her social worker called to postpone the visit with Emma today due to the growing concern for the virus. As a rule, She didn't watch the news in the morning because it was always negative and 90% political. She remembered hearing something about a virus spreading when the news was on last week, but didn't think much about it. They had not had any virus cases at the house so She hadn't thought it was a big deal. Diana said they would resume visits next week at the sober house so She wasn't too upset.

On the last night before moving to the sober house, She chose to stay in for the meeting, wanting to be with her friends. Ten minutes into the meeting, a new woman named Megan, who had arrived earlier that day, got up and stormed out of the meeting.

She overheard the staff calling out to Megan, and her response back, telling them to fuck off.

Instinctively, She got up and went outside to talk to Megan. She remembered her first night listening to people sharing about being happy, joyous, and free and how she had wanted to punch someone. If She'd had more courage she would have told someone to fuck off too. Megan was in the backyard pacing back and forth, trying to light a cigarette.

She went over and offered her a light. For a moment, She wasn't sure if she was going to get punched.

"There's no way I'm staying in this house. Everyone's crazy," Megan yelled.

She tried to ask her a question and Megan just continued ranting, "My mother was going to section me to a locked facility if I didn't come here, and if I leave, she *will* section me… the bitch." Meghan continued, "Maybe I'll just leave the state and find my friends in New York," Megan paced in circles. "I only overdosed once and don't see what the big deal is. The door's not locked; the door's not locked." Megan kept repeating to herself.

She took a chance while Megan was taking a drag on the cigarette and commented, "Maybe since the door's not locked, you could *choose* to stay just for the night and leave tomorrow if you still want to."

Megan stopped pacing and looked at her as if just now realizing someone else was there. "Why are you even out here talking to me, trying to trick me like the rest of them? What's in it for you?"

She took a step closer to the almost six-foot tall woman, and took a chance, "I felt the exact same way my first night and promised myself I would leave in the morning. Then morning came and I kind of liked getting a good night's sleep, having hot coffee in the morning, and nobody was trying to convince me to stay. Somehow it became my decision and that felt better. I am not trying to convince you of anything. It's just late and you must be tired. You can just go to bed. The staff have no way of forcing you to go back into the meeting."

They sat in the backyard for a long time. She took it as a good sign that Megan wasn't pacing or yelling anymore. She just sat with her in the big dark cold backyard. She thought of it as simply holding the space for someone, which Diana talked about in a group when someone was struggling. Inside, the meeting ended and the women started coming out back to smoke. They were all talking and laughing.

"Where's Room 23? I'm tired, sick and tired," Megan finally said.

She woke up on her moving day to pouring rain and thunder. *Kind of perfect*, She thought, *Going out with a real bang*. Her tiny single room was all packed up for the next person to make their own safe space. She remembered the nights of having faith that other people had faith in her until she could really believe in her recovery. She had survived – letting go of her boyfriend, her family meeting, first visit with Emma, Grampy's death, losing a friend, wanting to leave and run many times, her sister's suicide attempt, and really facing herself.

She stretched out on the bed and thought about Anna's death. She said a silent prayer and decided to walk to Anna's old room. A new young woman was in the room unpacking her suitcase. She felt a strong sense of hope for this woman's chance at a new life.

"This was once Anna's room," She said. "You would have liked her."

"That's weird. My name is Annie," The new girl replied, her long blonde bangs almost covering her eyes.

She didn't tell her about Anna's passing, just smiled and said, "Give this house a chance; it will change your life."

She took one last look through her bedroom and found a folder in her desk with her name on it. It was her photography project from an art group. She had forgotten all about it. Every week for a month, her art group walked around the grounds with iPads, taking pictures of things in and around and outside the house. Anything that sparked interest worked. Her first picture was of the large granite front steps leading up to the mansion. In art class, they were taught to use an app that allowed them to artistically change and enhance pictures to convey how they felt. She used shadowing to make the area around the steps look cloudy, made the stairs look like they were made of glass, and filled the windows in the house with light. Kind of like a haunted house, but a light-filled somewhat-happy haunted house.

She had taken six pictures in total that told her story from addiction to recovery. Her favorite was a picture of the house in the reflection of a puddle with autumn leaves around it. Each woman in the class had to present their project to the women and staff when the project was complete. She remembered feeling the strangest mix of terror and pride as she stood up to share her project. Looking back on it now, She smiled with a strong, calm sense of contentment that she had *stuck and stayed* through it all and was living a life in recovery.

Dear Emma, I love you! I am leaving soon to go to the sober house and we will be able to visit the playground. You can wear that nice puffy coat Nana got you and I will push you on the swing. I will still be living with other women in recovery in order to have a support system in place when I leave. I am looking forward to going for walks, having coffee with friends, getting a job, and mostly, seeing you soon! We will be able to see each other more and, after a couple of months in the sober house, we will be together. I am making changes and practicing being the best Mom I can for you.

Love you to the moon and back, Mumma

Hope

Judy came up to her room before the morning group and told her Diana needed to see her immediately. She giggled as the old thought popped into her mind, *Am I in trouble?*

Diana informed her that the sober house had called and they would not be taking transfers until further notice, due to an outbreak of the virus at the sober house. She froze, which she had not done in a while, and looked at Diana confused.

"The director has approved of you staying at Everson until the bed at the sober house opens," Diana assured her.

She was relieved that they hadn't already filled her bed and that she could stay longer; but the news about the virus spreading worried her. She realized how much her head had been in the sand over the past few months. She hated all the political drama on the news and hadn't cared to read anything online during her precious phone time. Listening to music, guided meditations, talking to her family and sponsor took up all her time. She walked back up to her room and looked at her bags all packed on her bed, feeling disappointed but grateful. Things not going her way didn't seem to topple her over emotionally anymore which was nice. When She saw the new women getting all freaked out over small things it helped her notice how much she had grown. She had compassion for them.

After dinner, She made a point of watching the news in order to catch up with what was happening with the virus. Her Mom hadn't really said much about it either, but then again Mom was the queen of head-in-the-sand living. The national news was focused on a New York hospital where the virus was spreading and they didn't have enough hospital beds. How had She possibly been so clueless to this?

Later, She talked to one of the RA's, who said the President had been downplaying it and saying it was like a flu and it would die down soon. Apparently over the past couple of weeks, it had gotten much worse and people were dying. She felt like she could never believe what the news was saying and asked for a computer pass so she could go online and do some research.

She didn't want to freak out any of the other women but, during the next in-house meeting, She asked if anyone had heard how bad things were getting in New York. Her sponsor Kate happened to be there and said she had heard a mask mandate was coming soon. Maybe even some sort of travel ban. Some of the women talked about how easy it was to be in a bubble in treatment and focus so much on yourself and the work you are doing, but that they all needed to stay educated.

Life on life's terms, She thought, *The whole world is dealing with the same thing, this a big one.*

"A Worldwide Pandemic May Be On the Way," one of the more reliable medical sources headlined, as she browsed online. She called Big Sis that night from the payphone to see how she was doing out there. Big Sis said her sober house had stopped taking new women that week too because of the concern for the virus. The residents were being asked to wear masks anytime they left the house and everyone got big bottles of hand sanitizer.

"How are you dealing with it?" She asked.

Big Sis sounded a little shaken up, "My biggest worry is that meeting attendance will shut down, and then what? The morning meeting is my saving grace and recovery anchor every day."

She hadn't even thought about that and realized how blessed she was having meetings right here in the house every night. She felt removed from reality in some way and couldn't manage to let dreaded guilt seep in, which always led to shame. Diana once made the distinction saying, *Guilt is feeling like you did something wrong and shame is feeling like you are wrong.*

She wrote in her journal that night about progress not perfection and not being so hard on herself. She loved the idea of someday, when Emma was older, giving her a mother's journal. The journal helped her to feel connected during their separation. She hoped it would help Emma understand why they had to be apart.

She thought often about what she had learned about the genetic component of addiction and knew Emma might have the genetic cards stacked against her due to both of her parents being addicts.

Wait.

Hold it.

Stop.

Yes.

There is relief and support in accepting the reality of my addiction as a real part of me. Not all of me, but something I am not ashamed of anymore, She thought.

"I am an alcoholic and an addict in recovery!" She said out loud.

With acceptance of her *disease* came a humble confidence that She could remain on course with her new healthy life as a woman in recovery and with showing Emma the right way. She would be honest with Emma about the struggles that her parents had. She would educate her on healthy coping skills instead of reaching for destructive ones. She loved the idea of teaching Emma to meditate and pray so that she never felt alone or hopeless in need of numbing the world out. The gratitude practice Diana had taught her was growing. Sometimes She felt gratitude and other times she *chose* gratitude, even when it was nowhere in sight. She wished her Mom and sister had these tools. *How weird that my life had to sink so low and almost lose it all to gain these tools*, She thought. It was as if She got mini-miracles every day that helped her deal with this Life on life's terms. She never would have been able to handle any of this alone and could have *been* another tragedy, if she'd still been out there in self-destruct mode. The thought of not being there for Emma made her sick to her stomach, like a near-miss deadly car accident.

The next morning, She enjoyed listening to everyone in PDMA and gave some feedback to the newcomers. She really understood why people in the program said the newcomer was the most important person. Hearing the raw touch-and-go, emotional, spiritual, and physical challenges of early recovery brought a deep sense of gratitude for the work She had already done.

She was the last to share that day. She took a deep breath.

"I am a grateful recovering alcoholic and addict." She said with confidence. "My name is Hope."

Dear Emma, I love you! It looks like I am going to have to stay at Everson a while longer due to a virus that is spreading and things are shutting down. I talk to my social worker and Nana every day so that I know what is going on with you. It is scary hearing about what is happening, but I truly have faith that we will get through this healthy and be stronger on the other end.

The real importance of community and support has become so clear to me, and I am grateful, even though things have taken a weird turn. I have learned that truly seeing and accepting my challenges is what helps me take solid steps towards change and getting better. For so long I had been afraid of who I had become in my addiction. The nice people here have helped me realize that you cannot change something if you are not being honest with yourself about it.

I am going to try and set up weekly FaceTime calls with you until we can see each other in person. I hope you're enjoying the book I wrote for you. I have started writing again and it makes me feel stronger and more sure of who I am every day.

Love you to the moon and back, Mumma

Pivot

"Good morning, my name is Hope. I am a grateful alcoholic in recovery." She shared the next day in a group meeting, smiling as women left for their next activities. "Everyone have a good day."

Noticing one of the new women grumbling under her breath, Hope added, "It gets better, don't quit before the miracle, as my Big Sis used to tell me."

Hope saw Judy standing in the doorway smiling, and appreciated that the staff had believed in her until she could believe in herself.

The smell of warm muffins filled the air as Hope headed outside, sipping her coffee, and settling under her favorite beech tree. She looked up at the bare branches reaching towards the sky. *Do the trees have a choice to reach upwards? Seems like they follow their nature, their inner knowing. Maybe that's why I have always loved trees*, She thought. *They have been trying to tell me something all along.*

In the Unity Group that day, Anne informed them that due to the growing pandemic concerns they would not be taking new admits until further notice. Consequently, most sober houses had stopped taking transfers. As well, community Twelve Steps Meetings were moving from in-person to Zoom only.

"You are all welcome and encouraged to remain at Everson until things stabilize," Anne assured the women. "We will keep you updated on any new developments. This is new territory for everyone."

Hope was the first to speak, "As intense as this all is, I am grateful to be at Everson and not isolated out there, so thank you."

"You can't lock us in here," Kara, who had only been there a few days, demanded.

"The doors aren't locked. If anyone chooses to leave, we will help you set up aftercare. I urge you not to make a snap decision based on emotions. This is overwhelming for everyone. It might help to talk about it in PDMA."

Other women had questions about appointments they needed to go to, court dates, and visits with their children. Hope already knew Social Services didn't want to bring children into a community setting but didn't say anything. She figured it would only be a couple of weeks till things would go back to normal.

"Recovery is a way of life, not a thing you do," Anne offered. "We will all get through this a step at a time, together."

"Let's focus on *what's not wrong*," Diana suggested.

This question kind of hurt Hope's brain, but also intrigued her. It seemed like another way to ask the *What's better?* question.

"I'm at Everson." Jen answered.

"Can you explain?" Diana asked.

"I'm safe, have all of my needs met, and I'm sober today," Jen affirmed.

Another woman named Sarah shared, "We're all together. Last week, we talked about the importance of staying connected as a foundational recovery tool. Can we say a prayer for the people out there that are afraid and isolated?" Sarah urged, "We will all get through this together."

The pandemic news became a regular event with morning coffee. New York was in a two-week lockdown and people were being asked to stay at home. Countries in Europe had police patrolling the streets, just making sure people didn't go outside. The safe walls of Everson suddenly never looked so good. Two weeks came and went with only worsening news about the virus. This was not the outcome many had predicted and it had certainly not *gone away*.

Hope kept in touch with Mom and Brenda daily. They were still able to see Emma which helped Hope deal with not being able to see her daughter right now. Her social worker wasn't sure how long visitation to programs would be suspended and it depended on what happened with the virus. Hope felt overwhelmingly powerless at times, sinking into it's-not-fair thinking, but she was surely not alone.

All of the women and staff at Everson were dealing with situations they had never been through before and Hope knew everyone was doing their best. Since they couldn't go out to community meetings and no commitments were coming in, the women were getting to know each other and growing closer every day.

By the third week with no new admissions, no discharges, and no visitors, they began getting creative about everything. Many women who were supposed to have completed the program were getting restless during the house meeting.

"I need to get back out there and help my Mom with my kids," Sarah commented during the house meeting.

"Would that be a supportive environment for your recovery?" Judy asked.

"No, my stepfather drinks like a fish; but I can't just sit here. Schools have just closed and my Mom has to figure out how to get my kids to do Zoom school. It's insane!"

"Think beyond your own situations and feelings and realize that the whole world is dealing with this crisis," Judy suggested to the group.

"My sponsor Kate told me all of the local meetings are now virtual only, and she is really concerned for the safety and well-being of people in early recovery that need the support of the group in person," Hope offered.

"I hadn't even thought about not being able to go to meetings," Sarah admitted. "I just feel so helpless."

Judy asked for raised hands of people feeling triggered by all of this, and most of the women slowly raised their hands.

"We should have Spirit Week next week and pick fun themes for every day," Stephanie suggested, trying to lift the spirits of the house.

The newest mother, Kim, had arrived at Everson with her baby, Caroline, a week before the shut- down. She had originally been told she had to remain in treatment at least three months and reach all of her treatment goals before she would be eligible to get custody of her baby back. Kim seemed very anxious about the virus and had confided in Hope that she was going to try and get Social Services to let her leave Everson early. Hope was worried about Kim and her sweet daughter. Caroline was very quiet and didn't make eye contact when people tried to get her to laugh or play. Kim was always handing her off to other women despite her reported fear of the virus. She was naturally pretty; but seemed more interested in doing her makeup and gossiping than being with her daughter. It seemed like Kim might be using the pandemic as an excuse to leave early. Hope overheard her on the phone talking to her boyfriend about getting a place together even though he was in treatment at the men's program.

Hope felt very protective of the babies at Everson because they were so innocent and perfect. She also realized she was jealous that Kim got to be here with her baby. When Kim shared her story in the Heart of the House Meeting she mentioned that Caroline was taken away from her when she was one-month old because she had overdosed. Hope felt a special connection to Caroline and wanted her to have the best chance at a happy life. She spoke to Diana about her concerns and Diana asked her to share her concerns with Kim. Hope was willing to at least try.

"Just share your own experiences," Diana encouraged.

After PDMA, Hope asked Kim, "Do you want to get a babysitter and walk the Trace trail after dinner?"

"Why?" Kim answered looking annoyed.

"I just want to get to know you better."

"Okay." Kim reluctantly agreed, walking away as she spoke.

"Meet me out front at 5:30." Hope called after her.

She wasn't surprised when Kim didn't show up after dinner, so she started walking alone.

"Hey, hold up," Kim yelled, catching up with her in the backyard. As soon as they started walking together, Kim started complaining about everything about the program. She seemed to have an issue with all of the staff and most of the other mothers in the annex.

"Nobody knows what I have been through, so who are they to tell me what to do with my baby?" Kim said repeatedly.

Kim was clearly shut down and angry. Hope was not sure how to approach her. She thought about what Diana said about sharing her own experiences, "I felt the same exact way my first month here. Most of the time, I thought the staff was trying to trick me into doing things and, most days, I thought about leaving."

Kim grew quiet, slowing down as Hope talked.

"What kept me here was my three-year-old daughter and wanting to be a better mother for her." Hope shared.

"I have always been a good Mom." Kate snapped.

Hope nervously shared, "I told myself I was a good Mom, even in my active addiction. As painful as it was doing the assignments and listening to other women, I realized that when I was in my addiction I couldn't be a good mother. Eventually, I couldn't take care of my child physically or emotionally."

Kim walked quickly back to the house without saying a word.

At least I tried. I'll pray for Kim and Caroline, Hope thought.

Hope wrote in her journal for a long time that night. She wanted to write until she figured out exactly what she did to find real motivation to change and embrace her recovery. Where was the turning point? What was the moment that she gave herself the chance at a better life? She needed to figure it out so that she could pass it on to Kim. She couldn't bear the feeling in her gut that Kim might fool her social worker and take sweet Caroline out too soon into a crazy world with no chance of being okay. She looked back over her journal, thumbing through the pages all the way to her first days at Everson. Hope was impressed with how honest she had been about her feelings, like how she didn't deserve a better life. In her addiction, it had become normal to accept abuse from other people, as well as herself, because she hadn't known a better way existed. It seemed like being honest about her misery and self-loathing opened a door for changes in her attitude, willingness, and then her behavior and choices. She would try one more time to talk to Kim.

Dear Emma, I love you so much! I know I have apologized for not being able to be the best Mom to you for the last year. I will continue to make it up to you in small and big ways, my sweet girl. I'm not beating myself up anymore though. I just didn't know what I didn't know and now, through the work I'm doing and through talking with other women, I understand that I am not a bad person. I didn't mean to make the mistakes I made and didn't have the skills, as my counselor says, to recover.

Love you to the moon and back, Mumma

Surrender

Hope had really been looking forward to meditation with the Buddhist monk on Friday and was disappointed when she found out he was on vacation. Maria put on a guided meditation CD for the group to listen to. Hope was glad to see Kim attending meditation even though she heard her joking about just wanting out of the health education group. The man's voice on the recorded meditation had an Australian accent; it was a very smooth relaxing voice. He led them through a body relaxation exercise journey to meet their higher selves. As they ascended to a space of pure light and warmth, bathing in liquid sunlight, they were introduced to their divine higher self. Hope felt like she was floating and felt tears streaming down her face, tears of coming home to herself where she was safe and purely loved.

His smooth voice facilitated a meeting, speaking on behalf of the higher self, "Welcome home, little one, I have been waiting for your return."

Hope was overwhelmed with feelings of a universal love, not attached to anything or anyone, just perfectly whole.

He softly continued, "You have journeyed a long way and have been through many challenges to make your way back to your true original spark of life."

Hope felt a loving warmth in her chest slowly moving through her body and felt like she was floating.

"Stay a while," he whispered. "Your higher self has your best interest at heart and has messages for you."

She drifted into the quiet, into the light. She had no concept of space or time when she heard the man's voice inviting her to say goodbye for now to her higher self and come back into the present moment in the room. Hope did not want to say goodbye to her higher self, but the man said they could connect again to their higher self whenever they wanted to. Hope trusted that the light would be there for her when she returned and slowly opened her eyes.

Diana came to the backyard and sat next to Hope under the beech tree, "I never chase people but are you okay?"

Hope looked at Diana with tears streaming down her face. They sat for almost five minutes quietly as Hope wept.

"This seems like healing," Diana offered, putting her hand on Hope's arm.

Hope took a deep breath, "I'm sorry, I'm sorry, I'm sorry." She felt unconditional love in the light with her higher self, "I'm so sorry for running from life for so long, from myself. Now, I finally feel the love of a mother, sister, father, daughter, friend. I feel the love of my own self and my connection to everything. But I don't want to lose …" Her voice trailed off.

"Lose what? "Diana asked.

"It's like there was this wall around me that I had put up for protection," Hope found her words, "and I rose up above the walls to this magical place, a place inside of myself. This is what I don't want to lose."

Diana suggested she keep journaling what she was experiencing.

During lunch, Kim came over to her table, asking if she could sit down. Hope was glad to see her as she motioned for her to sit next to her.

Kim looked her in the eye, "I'm sorry for being an asshole the other day. I know I have to be a better person and so I want to start with an apology."

Hope smiled knowingly, "The meditation, right?"

Kim nodded, "Yeah! What happened this morning? I've never meditated before. Is it always like that? Who was that guy? Did you feel like you HAVE to be a better person after that?" Kim asked with rapid fire insistence, like she had just woken up from hibernation.

Hope put her hand on Kim's, "It's going to be okay. You have plenty of time to figure it all out."

She told Kim about the energy healers, "There is definitely something amazing about working with the light and connecting to it during meditation. I never thought I would be able to meditate." Hope shared, realizing her progress.

Kim was curious about what she meant by *the light.*

"It feels like openness, hope, and this warm connection to … well, love." Hope expressed. "When I spend time with my Emma and your sweet Caroline I feel the light very strong in their innocence, like their souls are clean and fresh. That innocence connects with something in me, the light."

Kim looked at the ground, "I've been afraid to really connect with my daughter, in case I screw this up again and lose her. If we get close and then have to be apart again she would be devastated and I would not survive that again."

Hope took a quite deep breath, understanding the truth and weight of what Kim was feeling. "Through meditation, I learned the only time I truly have is right *now*. Looking to the future with fear robs me of getting stronger and trusting myself to do the right thing today."

"I am tired of being afraid of everything, including myself." Kim confided.

Hope remembered something helpful she had heard at the women's Twelve Steps Meeting: *When we are at the end of what we can do, that is when our higher power is finally able to step in and help, if we ask.*

Hope recognized the fight-or-flight look in Kim's eyes when she mentioned a higher power.

Kim paused, thinking about it, then said, "I'll do anything, I have to."

In the house meeting that week, Judy handed out surgical masks telling the women that they were not being required to wear them; but if anyone felt uncomfortable due to increasing virus cases in the county, they were available. Many of the women mentioned how strange it was to watch the morning news and see what a scary mess the world was. Also, how strange but good it felt to be safe and protected here with 40 women.

"The staff are all taking the recommended precautions with masks and hand sanitizer," Judy assured.

“I call to check in with my family every day, wanting to make sure they are safe and taking precautions,” Hope observed. “When I hear the anxiety in their voices I realize, maybe for the first time, that I am not only thinking about myself and what I need. Before all of this, I would have told you I was not self-centered anymore but I was. Now, I know what it's like to truly think and care about others and not just myself or my self-pity. All of us are going through this.” Hope looked around to see almost all of the women nodding in agreement.

“As things in the world are getting worse, I'm worrying about my parents who are taking care of my kids. I feel embarrassed about how selfish I’ve been, demanding they come visit every weekend, bring me cigarettes, and put *my* needs first,” Andrea shared.

Other women commented that they realized the same thing.

It had been a month since the world had locked down but the house seemed stronger than it had been in four months, Hope realized. A palpable presence of gratitude even through the challenges seemed to affect everyone, including the staff.

During the first Spirit Week, everyone dressed up for the theme of the day, including Friday Pajama Day. Hope’s favorite was Hippie Day. She was amazed at the creativity to make costumes from what was in the house. It felt like a sober party every day. They had a dance party, karaoke, and take-out pizza night.

The Saturday morning news program brought a very somber mood to the house when they repeatedly showed an eighteen-wheeler refrigerator truck parked outside of a New York hospital for the bodies of people that had died from the virus.

“I feel guilty for having so much fun this week while so many innocent people are dying,” Pam shared in PDMA. “I overdosed seven times and shouldn’t even be here.”

“Why shouldn’t you be here?” Diana asked softly.

"I used opiates, knowing I could overdose and die; so it was my own fault!" Pam yelled, "I have friends that overdosed one time and died. Why me? Why did I survive?"

"That sounds like survivor's guilt. If you both went through something and you survived, it leads people to believe they don't deserve to be alive if someone else died. Do you think there is purpose in your life today?" Diana asked. "Here you are, making changes, being an example, and being of service to other people in early recovery."

Pam just sat with her head in her hands.

Hope shared, "Prior to being at Everson, my life felt like a burden and I didn't know why. I always felt like I was wandering through life; like everyone else seemed to know what they were doing. One of the most helpful things I have learned is that everyone struggles, not just people with addiction. Recovery offers a way to deal with struggles with the support of people doing the same thing."

Hope looked over at Pam who had lifted her head from her hands and seemed to be listening.

Hope continued, "I know that my purpose - one of my purposes in life - is to connect with other people and share my spark of life. I know I can find and use my purpose to help others. I've always looked backwards with regret and forward with fear. Now that I can be present and not frozen, I can make real decisions about my life. I know there will be times I'll be afraid, but I don't have to run or numb myself to deal with it. I'll make mistakes; we all do, but no mistake is final as long as I don't pick up a drink or a drug, no matter what." Hope paused. "There is not one thing in my life that a drink is going to make a damn sight better," Hope said with a smile. "An old timer at the morning meeting used to say every day, and it worked for him for 25 years!"

"I've always wondered why I'm still here." Another woman named Pam related, "I do feel better when I help the new women in the house; like maybe if I can help someone, I'm giving back."

Diana handed out a written assignment: *What Purpose Means to Me.*

During the daily FaceTime call with Brenda, Hope told Brenda how proud she was of her.

Brenda opened up, "Prior to my suicide attempt, I was sure I'd never figure out what I wanted to do or have the courage to follow through. I felt as if I could never do anything good enough. I put so much pressure on myself to try and be perfect. It seemed like other people had everything figured out. I felt lost and hopeless. Keeping my feelings a secret spiraled me lower and lower."

Hope was shocked to hear her sister's view of herself.

"I always looked up to you for having it all together. I was actually jealous, feeling like I couldn't measure up to you!"

"Exactly," Brenda said. "I was not allowed to ever be the messy one and had to make it look like I had it all together. Drinking helped ease the pressure but I couldn't do that to Mom after what you put her through, no offense." She noted. "I met a lot of amazingly strong people in the hospital and in the outpatient group. They had also lost their ability to see their potential and worth. I felt completely understood and could be honest about my darkest feelings and thoughts. That's where my hope really started to grow."

Hope had never felt so connected to her sister.

"I know I want to work with troubled children and really make a difference in their lives," Brenda shared.

They both realized that through their darkest times, not only had they learned to reconnect to their sense of selves, they had learned to reconnect to each other.

"Gotta turn my phone in soon," Hope shared. "I need to work on my assignment from Diana about finding my purpose."

"That's so weird; my counselor gave me an assignment on finding purpose yesterday. Let's do our homework and read it to each other tomorrow!" Brenda suggested.

Hope felt the rush of goosebumps and the synchronicity within this real connection with her sweet sister, Brenda.

Dear Emma, I love you! I feel inspired today, to take on new challenges and move forward. I heard the definition of courage is feeling fear and taking action despite the fear, even with fear as a motivator. Everyone really struggles, and we don't know what someone else is going through unless we ask. I want to and will be a better person and not just have superficial conversations with people anymore. The morning meeting I go to is called Each Day, a New Beginning. It's true. If we have a perspective of starting fresh every day and not dragging emotional baggage from day-to-day, we get a clean slate to make the changes we want. When I was little and acted cranky, Grampy would always say, "Good morning!" No matter what time of day it was, telling me to start the day over. He was onto something, for sure. Can't wait to see you and hug you, my sweet pea. Love you to the moon and back, Mumma

Purpose

What purpose means to me: Purpose is the cumulative effect of meaningful goals. Purpose is a less tangible, long-term aim or guiding principle based on meaning. It's the impact we want to have on the world. I don't think I ever thought about goals or anything long-term with much meaning. Once I found the off-switch of alcohol for my overall discomfort with life, that was my only goal, to not feel. And it worked. The alternative to numbness seemed to be confusion, shame, pain, anxiety, worry, and feeling like I didn't belong. When I was numb, Life was easier, manageable. I understood why people drank and was sure I had found my way.

I always loved books, both reading and writing. And I loved my dog. Both were unconditional, constant, and loving. As soon as I could spell, I wrote and illustrated a book called Walking My Dog about a girl who started a dog-walking business. Throughout the darkest times in my addiction, I wrote, trying to find a way out… or a way in. I always felt a connection in the company of an open, blank page, awaiting my words.

When Emma came along, I prayed I had found my purpose in her sweet innocence and perfection. But I still didn't have the support or coping skills to be real, to be present in my life. When I screwed that up, my most sacred purpose it seemed, I think I gave up completely. But I prayed and wrote. Looking back on my journals, I was writing prayers, begging that God – Someone, Something, Somewhere – would listen. I had accepted that I had no purpose. Now, in recovery, I accept the challenge of exploring what my purpose is.

And here I am now, writing. And I know there is a Higher Purpose, I can feel it.

Hope sat at her little desk, in her cozy single room, on the third floor of this healing house, writing. She sensed she was exactly where she was supposed to be, finishing this assignment for Diana that she would share with Brenda tomorrow. Hope couldn't wait to hear Brenda's homework on finding purpose.

Feeling nostalgic, Hope pulled out her gratitude list notebook and read through it. It was surreal how much she had changed and grown in five months. She heard Judy's voice in her head. Some *people in their whole life never make the profound and lasting changes that people in recovery make.* What a blessing to be able to take time out of life's run-around, take stock of what is working and what's not, and take measured steps towards changing the parts that don't serve you. Most people don't critically examine where they are in life, set goals, measure steps towards goals, and readjust through action. PDMA! Some of the alumni came in for Commitment Meetings and shared how they still set a goal-for-the-day based on a challenge they are having.

Hope decided she would write a story about the work she did at Everson. The courageous women she had met, known, and learned from along the way. She loved the idea of setting this goal and giving herself a *purpose* that sparked passion in her. When she was writing, she always felt like she was in a creative flow beyond her own inspiration.

Hope checked in with her sober house weekly as requested by the manager. They were still not taking transfers, which was fine with her due to the virus. The world still seemed unpredictably stressful right now. She hadn't been able to see Emma in over a month. Hope was grateful that since her Mom's job was now remote, she had been able to get temporary custody of Emma. Now they all saw each other through FaceTime every day.

"Mom seems to have mellowed out and is actually going to therapy to deal with her own issues instead of always focusing on me." Hope shared with Diana during their session.

"Do you think Mom's changes have anything to do with yours?" Diana asked in her curious Diana way that both confused and intrigued her at the same time.

"I did tell Mom that I am taking the reins of my recovery and my life and that I hoped she could focus on what makes her happy for once. Why do you ask?" Hope wondered.

"It's interesting to notice how when one person in the family starts to heal, it can be a power of example," Diana observed.

"I am nowhere near Step Eight and Nine which deal with making amends, but I am holding onto what Kate says about amends being about changes not apologies. Every day, I'm making small changes that are starting to heal the damage that my addiction caused myself and my family. If this helps my Mom in any way, I am grateful," Hope said.

That night one of the RA's found a live online guided meditation as an option to the Zoom Twelve Steps Meeting. Zoom meetings were very distracting though. Everyone missed the in-person commitments. During the meditation, after getting into a relaxed state, the woman in the Zoom session guided you up through the clouds, higher, higher up into the sky, drifting safely higher still above the ozone. Once there, you were guided to see the earth orbiting and view all of the countries of the world – our sacred, troubled, sick world. She explained that an illness had fallen upon all countries and cultures which spread through the air and touch. People had to separate and quarantine in order to unplug from the hectic day-in and day-out routines. Families had to stay at home and reconnect, the ozone was healing due to people working at home instead of commuting, and world health organizations were working together for a cure for us all. She guided us into visualizing our own life force as a bright light, a beacon, and then told us to bathe the earth with this bright warm light.

She said, "Cover the earth completely as it rotates, time after time, with loving healing energy. Feel the connection as we heal as one, no longer separate or able to justify that *it won't happen to me.* When you feel you have spread your love and light around the whole earth and filled in all of its needs, slowly come back down, through the clouds, further down, until your feet gently reach the earth. Each of us *in* the solution and in unity *is* the way towards healing." She finished.

Hope wrote the meditation in her book that night under a chapter she titled "Unity."

Finally, that morning there was *good news* amidst the daily tragic news of the rising virus death toll. A vaccine was in trials and had been approved. There would be a push to get all healthcare workers vaccinated over the next week. This seemed like a turning point. Maybe things would start opening up. Other countries had already started giving vaccines and were lifting some of the restrictions. Hope was still bothered by the news and how much it seemed to thrive on blaming or dividing people, depending on which channel you watched. If ever there was ever a time to all pull together, it had to be now. Hope thought, *How helpful would it be if the news broadcasted the Unity meditation?*

Two months of the pandemic now and people were more restless. A couple of the mothers had moved on to smaller family programs due to the concerns about living with 40 women during a pandemic. The only babies left in the program were Jackson and Caroline. It seemed lonely in the annex with four of the Moms gone. Social Services were not placing babies in residential settings right now. Hope tried to spend as much time as she could babysitting. The babies seemed to be changing and growing before her eyes; it helped her not to feel so bad about not being able to see Emma. She often wondered what it was like for the babies when they left after living in a place where they were adored by so many women. Hope would joke with the mothers, saying their babies would have the best self-esteem since they experienced such a big fan club between the 40 residents, the staff, and the volunteer babysitters.

It was bizarre that this pandemic was the *new normal*. She had hated that saying but realized it was true. *Normal* would continue shifting as the world figured out how to move safely forward.

Thursday afternoon, the women were invited to attend a special poetry group with a guest speaker named Ada. She was an established poet and had to be close to 90-years-old. They hadn't had any volunteers for over two months; but Ada came in wearing a mask, "Poetry is too important!"

Passion for a purpose, there it is, Hope thought, adoring her.

Ada talked about poetry as a whisper of our divine connection.

"If you have the call to write, listen, then write!" Ada affirmed.

Ada offered a free writing assignment: "Let Loose Your Pen." Ada said ever so poetically, "Let it dance with inspiration across the open page."

As a teenager, Hope once did a long distance walk with her uncle. The memory and the words and images poured out of her into a poem.

Putting the pen down, she hoped Ada would like it.

Calling

I discovered and lost you upon those winding roads.
Pain danced amongst the shadows between suffering and acceptance.
Limits rose and fell with each step, silently transforming.
Time lost meaning amidst open spaces that respected not our frailty.
Without expectation or cause, boots on the trail, I discovered.
Choice became necessity as the road spread out before me.
In my weakness, You Are Strong, ringing through rising up.
Where my feet would land at times was all I could see.
Until lifted up, the sky welcomed my fear and translated it to wonder.
Wonder of this land and my presence among its history and mystery.
Its mystery now woven through my soul, calling to my spirit's purpose.
Now as I travel the roads familiar, an unfamiliar traveler.

> *Dear Emma, I love you! I am so glad we get to talk to each other on the phone. I love hearing about your day and seeing how big you're getting. You are going to be tall like your grandfather. I miss him and wish he was here to see how amazing you are! I talk to him every day when I say my prayers and I know he is looking out for us both. I feel really strong and I don't worry so much about what is going to happen next.*

There have been so many times that I have been afraid but I had faith that things were going to work out, and I did the next right thing.

That's something they talk about here – keeping it simple, just taking the next right step, and not worrying about the next ten steps. It's really nice having people understand how you feel and share their experience of how they deal with challenges. We truly don't have to be alone, unless we choose to be. I love thinking about you reading this journal someday. I will be there to answer any questions you have and support you always. You are a gifted, spirited, beautiful soul and I am the luckiest Mom in the world.

Love you to the moon and back, Mumma

Moving On

Two and a half months into the quarantine, Hope got a message from the sober house manager that they were accepting transfers and there was a bed for her next week. She felt a calm assurance that things were going to work out this time.

"The time has come to move on," Hope shared during her PDMA check-in.

"How does it feel? 'Diana asked.

"Respectful, confident," Hope humbly answered. "I know I don't have all of the answers for what lies ahead, but I trust that I know how to ask for and receive help now. Thank you all for your honesty, support, and for each of you being an amazing power of example. Every woman I have met has taught me something."

"What has been the most challenging recovery skill to learn?" Diana asked.

"The mess," Hope said simply. "The human condition is so messy, Anne is right, but in recovery I can accept where I am and get support. I realize it's rare to find people willing to really be honest. One of the biggest gifts of Everson has been the staff. Caring enough to help us see the truth no matter how painful. How to face it, make changes, and be able to do the same for other women. Other places I've been to didn't care enough to really challenge me to face the reality of my life. PDMA Rule Number Four, No sugar, No shit."

The women laughed at her paraphrase of *giving honest feedback based on observed behaviors.*

Hope continued, "When we didn't know what to do, the staff would stand beside us and help us learn. Like when I would not or could not admit that I'm an alcoholic and addict. For almost three months I fought that. The staff encouraged and supported me in finding my voice in my own time," Hope smiled.

With Diana, Hope called her Mom to let her know she would be moving on to the sober house next week. Mom wanted to check with Social Services to see if Hope could come home since she had been in treatment almost six months. Hope was shocked at this offer, not because it was not a good idea, she had just never even considered that option. A careful transition had been recommended and she felt she needed a structured step-down between Everson and home. *Wherever home was going to be.*

A pang of guilt rose up about her Mom having to take care of Emma, even though it was Mom's idea to take care of her when her work went remote.

"Are you being called back to work in person?" Hope asked.

"No, I just thought it would be nice to have you home," Mom replied.

Hope was used to feeling many conflicting feelings at once, but had to ask Mom if she could think about it and call her back tomorrow. She felt she needed to go to the sober house for at least a month, but didn't yet know how to assert herself. Hope thanked her Mom and hung up the phone. She stared at Diana in disbelief and a bit of fear, not having felt so torn in a long time.

"I don't want to disappoint my Mom and I want to be with Emma, but I feel guilty for no apparent reason. I just know the sober house is the next right step," Hope acknowledged.

Diana asked lots of questions.

All Hope kept coming back to was guilt.

"Feels like putting myself first is the wrong thing. Due to old guilt for being apart from Emma, guilt for my mother's unhappiness, on and on. It suddenly feels like a bottomless pit rising up out of nowhere, a sinkhole of sorts."

Hope realized she felt confidence, for the first time, within the recovery community. She was beginning to develop her strengths, was a senior peer in the house, and felt like a strong woman here. But, within the complicated layers of the relationship with her Mom, she felt her confidence slipping away. Mom had not done or said anything to guilt her; it was her own lingering sense that she had done something wrong, realizing she had felt this way since she was child.

"Do you trust your decision to go to the sober house?" Diana asked.

"Yes," She immediately replied without hesitation.

"Letting go of other people's expectations and ideas about what's best for you takes time and practice like all parts of recovery," Diana assured. "Seems like this would be a good time for you to journal and explore the many layers of guilt that are surfacing. Recovery has to be a balance of self-care and showing up for others, but it takes awareness and time. Healing is not linear; it's a spiral and we hit the same issues but move higher through the healing process as we go," Diana suggested.

Journal in hand, Hope found her way to her favorite tree on the edge of the backyard and sat beneath the tightly-budded branches. There was something so honest about the March trees. Their sprawling branches were stark against the blue sky, yearning for Spring's new growth. Birds flit from branch to branch, eager for the returning comfort of lush green leaves.

"It is what it is," she whispered, one of Mom's favorite sayings that used to annoy her, but made sense now. Certain things – like the simplicity of nature's changing seasons – *just are*. She flipped through her well worn journal, realizing it was almost full, only a few blank pages left. A feeling of satisfaction washed over her as she thumbed through its pages, honoring that each word was a stepping stone, closer to herself.

I Am, Hope wrote, beneath her favorite tree, with her favorite pen, in her favorite journal.

I Am, I Am, I Am ... a discovery of self.

That is recovery. That is life.

I am whole as I sit here, part of this tree, part of the clouds drifting across the blue sky, and the birds singing safely nestled above.

My spirit and soul are innocent and divine. May my life be a reflection always.

I am not the mistakes I have made as a daughter, sister, girlfriend, addict, or mother.

There is a life force within me whose purpose is in connection with others.

Dear Emma, I love you! I am so proud of you, and proud of me! It is time for me to move on and I know with all of my being that this is the right time. I have learned so much from each of my Everson Sisters. Each piece – large or small – that someone has shared with me has touched me and taught me. I know what it is like to have real friends who care about me unconditionally. Feels like another lifetime ago that I arrived here, so hopeless and scared. I never have to feel that way again.

Love you to the moon and back, Mumma

Grace

Hope opted for the Zoom Twelve Steps Meeting that night instead of the peer-led meeting. It was a speaker-led meeting and it would be good to sit and listen. Despite the online format, she felt very connected and grateful to have found such a welcoming community. A young man shared how desperate he was to get into treatment. For the past two months, he could not get a bed due to limited availability.

"I've never been more motivated to get sober, but all of my efforts are for nothing because day-after-day I can't stop using," he pleaded.

He had been in treatment when the pandemic hit and then left it, using the virus as an excuse not to be in community living. He asked for prayers from the group and said he would keep showing up and keep trying no matter what. Hope closed her eyes and said a prayer that a bed would open for the desperate young man, soaking in her deep gratitude for the opportunity and the grace she had been gifted.

At the end of the meeting they recognized and celebrated lengths of sobriety. Hope was shocked to see Big Sis get up to receive a 24-hour keychain. She must have relapsed, but Hope was grateful she was at a meeting getting help again. Hope had so many reminders that day to stay firmly planted in today's recovery - to keep it simple, honest, and humble.

Walking over to Diana's office for their last session, Hope thought back to the first time she walked into that office, remembering what an angry, terrified girl she had been. *Who was that girl?* Hope mused. *That girl was determined to get through treatment, get Social Services off her back, and nobody was going to make her change.*

Through honest listening, caring, and steadfast challenging, Diana had helped Hope open so many doors, clean house, and change how she thought and acted. She now had the strength and skill to make decisions, not just react out of self-destructive habits. She had compassion for herself, where not long ago she had only disdain.

"Thank you, Diana, for creating a truly safe space for me to heal and for never giving up on me when I wanted to give up on myself. You have shown me the way, day-after-day, to change my life," Hope expressed. "I have actually had moments of gratitude for the virus that stopped us all in our tracks. It challenged me to focus on what really, really matters. These past few months have single-handedly removed the distractions and illusions of what building a recovery foundation needs to look like for me. I hope Everson will keep most of these recent changes once the quarantine is fully lifted. They gave me a sanctuary with less distraction for my healing journey."

As she was walking out of the office, Hope turned back one more time, "The magic that everyone talks about?" Hope paused, "It is not in these walls, but in the unconditionally loving and committed staff who shine the light and lift us up to see our potential as women of dignity and strength in recovery."

Diana thanked her for her courage and beauty and reminded her that she could return for two weeks for the PDMA group as a supportive transition tool. Hope handed Diana a folder labeled, *As She Recovers.* The first two chapters of the book she started writing about Everson, The Healing House.

The morning of her moving day, Hope thought back to the first time she was supposed to go to the sober house, pre-pandemic. She was nervous and excited three months ago, unsure if it was true that you just needed to keep the same habits out there as you did at Everson, so that you would stay in recovery, a day at a time. This final day she felt grounded and strong in her faith that she had the tools and the habits in place to remain in recovery, no matter what.

Kate was coming to pick her up after PDMA and help her move into the sober house. Downstairs, Hope expressed her gratitude to her sisters in recovery and talked about how she had gained a real family.

"I never knew it was possible to be this close to anyone," Hope shared.

She reminded them of what Kate always told her, *you have to give it away to keep it.*

She was aware that she was about to be a newcomer in the sober house, which was going to have challenges of its own. More than anything, she looked forward to new growth opportunities. That Friday, Hope said her goodbyes to the staff and told them she would be back for PDMA the next Monday.

Standing on the front steps one last time as a resident, Hope felt the grace that her yoga teacher had talked about – the spontaneous, unmerited gift of divine favor. Here, Hope had been shown unconditional kindness, compassion, and love at her lowest point until she could find the motivation within her own spirit.

Walking down those four large granite steps, she whispered, "I've got this. The gift of desperation, willingness, and motivation… to take the next step, one at a time."

She turned to see the ivy, hints of green returning, still finding its way up the stone pillars, no matter what.

"Mumma!" She heard a familiar voice behind her and turned to see Emma running towards her just in time to catch her up in her arms.

"My baby!" Hope shouted, caught in a swirl of surprise, joy, love, and confusion that Emma was so big and grown up.

Hope felt another hug from behind and turned to see her Mom with a smile and tears in her eyes.

"I wanted to surprise you. It's been so long since you've hugged your Emma," Mom gushed.

Hope felt the spark of life move through her – and through her daughter – as she stood fully in this moment, in the shadow of the love of this healing house.

"I've got this," She whispered again, knowing that a day at a time, she would do what it took to keep this gift of recovery.

"Emma, let's go see my new house. It has a big backyard where we'll have our weekly visit and I will be able to visit you at home too! Then before you know it, I'll be home." Hope beamed.

Dear Emma, the best part of today, the best part of all of my days is seeing you! I love you! You are a shining star, a guiding light, my true joy. I'm glad you got to see my new room and help me make my bed. Nana told me that you are making your bed everyday, just like Mumma does.

There is so much we are going to learn and share, growing up together.

Love you to the moon and back, Mumma

Epilogue
End of an Era

Her transition to the sober house went smoothly. It was strange entering a world that was masked and socially-distanced. This was what the world was going through while she was quarantined with 40 women in the big beautiful mansion a mile from the beach. In her new freedom, she recognized her own strength and commitment as she kept the habits she had developed and maintained at Everson.

Hope brought her recovery rock with her to the sober house and made her own little recovery bowl full of beautiful crystals. Walking down the stairs of the sober house, she scooped her recovery rock from the crystal bowl and headed out to the backyard, where she'd found a new beech tree. Since they didn't have a recovery bowl at the sober house, Hope dedicated this beautiful tree in the backyard as her recovery foundation. Like the beech tree, she remained rooted and grounded in the earth, reaching for the light, and breathing.

"Help me stay away from a drink or drug today and if I feel vulnerable I will reach out for help." She whispered, standing beneath the sprawling branches full of new buds. She prayed and made a commitment to her recovery, no matter what, and looked forward to seeing everyone at PDMA.

That Monday morning, after her Twelve Steps Meeting, Hope arrived for the PDMA group. Everyone was gathered in the living room for the usual 9 am morning check-in with the Director; but it was 9:05 and Anne wasn't there yet. Anne was never late and the women were starting to wonder what was wrong. At 9:10, Anne walked in, all of the other staff filing in behind her. They looked very serious. Anne had always been very transparent with the community. She took a deep breath and looked at each of the women, "We always talk about dealing with Life on life's terms aka challenges. Well, we have another unforeseen challenge."

Anne informed the women that Everson was being shut down due to a lack of adequate funding to keep the program open. She shared specific information about the growing gap between what it costs per bed for the services Everson offers and what the state actually reimburses for those services. "Insurance companies don't cover extended treatment and we rely on state money which covers about one third of the cost per bed, per day," Anne shared.

Many of the women began crying. One of the women yelled out, "My insurance company covered twenty detox admissions last year. Why won't they pay for services that actually work to save people's lives?"

The women lodged questions at Anne and the staff, demanding answers.

"The program will not be closing until we are able to safely place everyone here. We will not be taking any new admissions." Anne said. "I can ask my supervisor to meet with you if that would be helpful,"

The women talked amongst themselves and decided to sign a petition to stop the closing. Anne assured them they would get through this together and that nobody would be without a plan.

"What about the mothers that need this place to heal and get their babies back?" Kim yelled. "There is no place like Everson. We have to fight for what is right!"

Anne encouraged them to write letters if they felt that would help and they could figure out where to send them. Hope looked around the room and could not imagine this house no longer being the house of miracles for women in recovery.

Hope tried to bring positivity to the group, "I know this is scary, but there is a really supportive community of sober houses when you leave. My heart breaks for the women who will not have the amazing opportunity we have all had here, together."

Sarah sat in front of the large fireplace with her head in her hands, murmuring, “I thought I built a strong foundation the first time I was here. I stayed sober 2 years, then I relapsed and lost everything, including my will to live. Knowing I could come back here and heal is the only reason I am still alive.”

“Yes,” Anne assured. “Addiction is a chronic disease. It is treatable. If you stop using the basic recovery tools and stop treating your addiction, relapse may happen. Each day is a new beginning. By learning and practicing recovery skills and staying connected to your support system, you have the power and the choice. *If* you do relapse, you have the knowledge of the tools. You need to humble yourself, ask for help, and take action.”

Hope agreed. “Even in the short amount of time I’ve been at the sober house, I realize my recovery is the choices I make every day. It is not attached to a building, a person, place, or thing.”

“Once Everson family, always Everson family,” Judy offered with confident peace.

Hope found the challenges she had during the week seemed to work themselves out through keeping in touch with her support network. Little by little, she didn’t feel like she *needed* PDMA to stabilize her. Maybe that was the goal of the PDMA bridge, to help women during their transition realize that they *do* have the coping skills needed to stay in recovery. She continued writing her story of Everson and looked forward to the day she could hand the finished copy to Diana.

She knew these were important chapters of her life that had unfolded during her six months in the healing house. Every woman she met and the thousands of women who had passed through the doors before her lived on in the house, in the staff and in the spirit of women supporting women. Hope read something on social media that rang true for her recovery process: *The woman I am now is much more sovereign in her power. She is aware and present and knows that what she puts out there, she creates. So she keeps creating, for the better not the worst, because she knows she is worth it.”*

On Hope's final day at PDMA, she asked if she could stay for the Unity Group one last time. Judy told her it would not normally be allowed but given the intensity of what was going on with the closing news, she would check with the director.

Instead of the usual healthy dark chocolate, Anne passed around a bowl of mixed chocolate with Snickers, Twix, and Almond Joy. All of the staff attended the meeting too because Anne said they were going to talk about transition plans and process the upcoming changes.

"Are there any questions before we get started?" Anne asked.

The room was eerily quiet and still.

"How are the staff doing with the closing?" Hope asked.

Anne accommodated the usual silence while she looked around at all of the staff in the room.

"Coming here every day, walking alongside the most courageous, strong, beautiful, creative women for over 25 years has been an honor and blessing," Anne affirmed, looking at each staff member and woman in the room.

Diana admitted, "I am learning to accept the news alongside these brave women. You are all an inspiration."

One by one, the staff shared.

Amelia teared up, "Thank you all for your courage in the face of this challenge. I have found strength walking through this uncertain time because we are going through it, together."

Bethany admitted, "I am still angry about the decision and I'm working on acceptance. My anger is helping me stay focused on helping others even though I know I need to feel the loss and be honest with myself."

Maria shared, "On my journey as an intern, recovery aid, and counselor, I have learned so much. Thank you all for showing up with courage as you learn to change and grow."

Then someone asked, "Where's Judy?"

Anne called Judy into the dining room asking if she wanted to share how she was feeling.

"Change is one of the most consistent parts of life, "Judy answered, looking over to Anne and stopping mid-sentence. Judy reached for one of the

God boxes – a box holding private notes of worries and concerns – which she had taught everyone to make during art therapy. "We never know when life is going to throw us a curveball. We all need spiritual connections." Judy paused as she reflected, "Watching women get the spark of life back in their eyes, their laughter, and their connections with each other has been such a blessing in my life."

Then Judy stood, trying to catch her breath, looking down at the *God box* in her hand.

"Everson women go out into the world carrying a message of hope and light," Judy shared. "I have faith that, through this loss and change, God has a plan and I need to continue choosing faith over worries and fear, day by day, minute by minute."

Anne thanked the staff and women for being honest and supportive, "I truly believe we have been together at this time to touch each other's lives and that these connections cannot be lost."

Hope thought about the Everson Alumni and realized how special this community truly was, even more so now. She felt a responsibility to carry the light and hope of Everson forward and not let the true message of healing in recovery stop, just because the building was closing.

In her gratitude for being able to stay for the Unity Group, Hope shared, "While I was here in my perfect little single room on the third floor, I started to write the story of Everson. It's called *As She Recovers*. I dedicate it to the Angels of Everson."

Dear Emma, heart of my heart, Emma. I wrote once about a card which said having a child is like having your heart walk around your body. You are my heart. Thank you for skipping and twirling joy into my life. This journey back to you has been the most challenging thing I have ever imagined I would be able to do. When you were born, I loved you so much that I was sure my love would motivate me to do the right thing and make the best choices for you; but I didn't understand yet how to make the right choices for myself, to really care about what I need to be the best me. Kind of like learning to care for myself as sweet little Hope, who was once innocent and afraid, lost and unsure. I had to learn to have enough courage to look at the choices that had hurt me, hurt you, and everyone I love, and begin to forgive myself. Living with other women that were doing the same work helped me realize I am worth it and I deserve a good life.

Growing up, my family did their best, but they didn't talk about feelings and how to handle the painful confusing parts of life. Life is challenging, for everyone, and sometimes people turn to alcohol and drugs as a way of coping with discomfort, confusion, and pain. I know that there are some things I won't be able to protect you from in life; but I can promise you that I now have the tools, the support, the self respect, and commitment to be there for you 100% as a sober Mom.

I have learned that in trying to hide from life's painful things, I was also hiding from life's wonderful things. Yes, there will be tough days. Maybe we will cry or not know what to do, but we can ask for help, laugh, have fun, love each other, grow, and make new memories.

An important part of recovery is having a spiritual connection. I struggled with this for a long time, feeling like a bad person for making bad choices. But I got to know other people who also made bad choices in their addiction, and I really felt they deserved a second chance at a happy life. As I connected to the other women here, I realized that I deserved that too. I opened up to nature's healing presence, allowing the wind, trees, sun, and ocean to remind me of my goodness. I connected to my Dad – your Grampy – and knew that he still loved me from the Great Beyond. I felt sad when my own Grampy died, but comforted that my Dad - your Grampy - would be there to greet him on the other side. I believed that others believed, seeing their faith get them through really hard times. I began trusting the staff at Everson, knowing that they only wanted me to get better and have a good life. I have friends in recovery who support me in my messy, confused times and in my happy times. I am never alone, and you, my sweet angel, will never be alone.

We have a lot of things to figure out, and we will do it together, as a family, with Auntie Brenda and Nana. I still pray that your Dad gets the help I was able to get. It's really hard to take that first step; but if I did it, anyone can. By reconnecting to my light through energy healing, I can recognize the light of others. I want to help other people find the way back, the way I have been helped. Even though we are not together, he is a good person. We can say prayers for him at night before bed.

The world has been through a rough time with the pandemic. I think we are all learning about making healthy choices and the importance of connection with the people we love. Just like we all adapted to things over the past few months with the quarantine, we will continue to adapt and make the best of things moving forward. Recovery is not a thing I do but a way of life. I want to be the best person I can be – for myself and for you, sweet Emma Noel. I am the best person I can be at this moment and can't wait to discover new things with you. Of course, I will make mistakes in life. We all do, but I will say I'm sorry if needed, ask for help, then make another decision.

Thank you for loving me and giving me the gift of being your Mom.

Each day truly is a new beginning.

Let's write our new story together, Hope and Emma Together!

Love, Mumma

Author's Note

Recovery is possible. If you – or someone you know – are suffering from addiction or wondering if alcohol or drug use is not serving your life, you are not alone, help is available.

The women's treatment program I led closed in July 2020; however, I am now co-founder of Shamballa Healing Center in West Falmouth MA, helping people rekindle their light, purpose, and joy through individual and group energy healing/mentorship programs.

Shamballa Healing Center
Website: www.shamballahealingcenter.com

The following resources are available for treatment options:

Alcoholics Anonymous
Website: www.aa.org
AA Hotline and Meeting info: 800-839-1686
Support for family members: https://al-anon.org

SAMSHA Hotline (Substance Abuse & Mental Health Services Administration)
Website: www.samhsa.gov & https://www.refugerecovery.org
Phone: 1-800-662-4357

Acknowledgements

For as long as I can remember, my three sons Colby, Myles, and Noah have always believed in, supported, and encouraged my love of writing. They asked me the question often, "Mom, when are you going to write your book?" You three infuse my life with joy, fun, and inspiration.

For my sweetest Rick, who loves, supports, and encourages my book-loving, tree-adoring, cloud-gazing, book-sniffing passions. Always my adventure partner and unconditional support, you expand my horizons with joy and love.

Endless gratitude for Team Emerson, the inspiration for this story. To the courage and strength of the women who allowed us into their healing journey with heart and soul. To the profoundly devoted women that worked side-by-side every day to guide, inspire, challenge, love, and light the way for the Emerson patients. Their dedication and steadfast commitment made the miracle of the healing house possible.

Deep gratitude to long-time friend and supporter Bill Dougherty, founder of Recovery Without Walls, who 26 years ago suggested I work in the recovery field. When I told Bill I was writing the story of Emerson he said, "What you created at Emerson cannot be replicated, and must not be forgotten." Thank you for cheering me on with honesty and love.

Emerson's Art Program and Angel Nina Webber for bringing creative healing support of the art program in honor of her daughter Jennifer, and her generosity and for editorial sponsorship.

Honored thanks to Anne Jolles for bringing The Grace Trail® to Emerson, which brought healing to hundreds of women.

The steadfast vision of "Friends of Emerson" Chair Martha Ross's commitment to the honor, dignity, and support of our healing mission.

The unconditional love and support of Mary LeClair, once Chair of the Board and forever friend and champion for women in recovery.

Wholehearted appreciation for the fierce support, love, and generosity of the larger community of donors that stepped up to help bring Our story to the world.

Light and Love to Ariana and Jordan Bain from the Modern Mystery School for bringing your healing energies and light to Emerson and to my life.

Gratitude for the gifted, talented artistry of Lulu Lovering Shepherd for the beautiful book cover design. You captured the essence and magic of *As She Recovers*.

The magical leadership and wisdom of my editor Sun Cooper, of Sun Literary, whose loving book shepherding helped bring my dream to reality.

And my foundation, my deepest gratitude to my parents for being their unconditional support and love.

Author's Bio

Angela Shepherd lives on Cape Cod with her family, where she continues to help people connect to their joy and purpose through her energy healing business, Shamballa Healing Center. Throughout her 25-year career leading a residential substance use and mental health treatment center, Angela has always believed deeply that people can and do recover and lead healthy, purposeful lives. Her approach to helping people find their inner strength is based in integrity and unity consciousness. Helping others truly begins with *walking the walk* ourselves. Angela is a person in long-term recovery, with an unwavering belief in all paths to healing. Her resilience and commitment to helping people sustains and inspires her to seek higher ways to engage individuals in stepping into their potential. As a Certified Healer through the Modern Mystery School, Angela supports anyone looking for more – more connection, purpose, joy, gratitude, and change. Angela's love of words, books, nature, hiking, wild weather and family continue to inspire her joyful creativity. She is currently working on the sequel to *As She Recovers.*

www.ingramcontent.com/pod-product-compliance
Lightning Source LLC
LaVergne TN
LVHW090512110826
845146LV00003B/825

* 9 7 9 8 2 1 8 2 4 0 7 5 2 *